30-MINUTE
HIGH PROTEIN LOW CARB
COOKBOOK FOR BEGINNERS

Burn fat, build lean muscle, and feel unstoppable energy.

Sarah Hollins

INDEX

WHO I AM	4
WELCOME: WHY THIS BOOK CAN REALLY HELP YOU	5
My Journey and Your Next Step	5
How to Make the Most of These Pages	5
HIGH PROTEIN, LOW CARB: DISCOVER THE BENEFITS	6
What It Really Means	7
Why It Can Help You Feel Lighter and More Energetic	9
A Simple Explanation of Proteins, Carbs, and Fats	10
Balancing Nutrients Without Stress	11
SAVE TIME WITHOUT GIVING UP FLAVOR	13
Smart Grocery Shopping	13
Handy Tools and Quick Cooking Methods	14
Meal Prepping Made Easy	15
Small Steps to Stay Motivated Day by Day	16
BEFORE YOU START COOKING: WHAT YOU NEED TO KNOW	18
What You'll Find in the Next Pages	19
Reading Ingredients and Following Instructions with Ease	19
Adapting Recipes to Your Needs	21
Getting Creative with Flavors	23
A WEEK OF IDEAS: MY SAMPLE MENU	24
Structuring Seven Days of Varied Meals	25
Tailoring the Plan to Your Daily Routine	30
RECIPES: THE BASICS BEFORE YOU HEAD TO THE STOVE	30
Making the Most of Your 30 Minutes in the Kitchen	31
Keeping an Eye on Protein and Carb Counts	32
FOOD VARIATIONS AND EATING ON THE GO	33
Simple Ingredient Swaps	35
Handling Social Events and Restaurant Dining	37
ENERGIZING BREAKFASTS	39
Sunrise Energy Omelette	40
Berry Burst Bliss Parfait	40
Green Glow Egg Muffins	41
Almond Dream Pancakes	41
Supercharged Morning Smoothie Bowl	42
Avocado Power Wrap	42
Cottage Crunch Sunrise Bowl	43
Turkey Twist Scramble	43
Chia Charge Overnight Pudding	44
Turbo Breakfast Burrito	44
Radiant Avocado Egg Bowl	45
Salmon Sizzle Toast	45
Nutty Berry Dream Yogurt	46
Flash Protein Smoothie	46
Zesty Zoodle Spark Stir-Fry	47
Dynamo Turkey Wrap	47
Ricotta Radiance Pancakes	48
Broccoli Boost Egg Muffins	48
Cottage Power Smoothie Supreme	49
Creamy Avocado Delight Salad	49
SIMPLE AND SATISFYING LUNCHES	50
Avocado & Turkey Power Bowl	51
Zesty Garden Chicken Wrap	51
Citrus Salmon Salad Sizzle	52
Quinoa & Veggie Boost Bowl	52
Spicy Shrimp Lunch Delight	53
Lean Beef Crunch Salad	53
Mediterranean Chicken Wrap	54
Tuna Tango Lettuce Boats	54
Greek Power Chicken Salad	55
Crispy Tofu & Kale Fiesta	55
Ultimate Turkey Cobb Wrap	56
Sassy Egg & Avocado Salad	56
Herb-Infused Chicken Zoodle Salad	57
Refreshing Shrimp & Cucumber Bowl	57
Lean Turkey & Spinach Power Wrap	58
Hearty Quinoa Veggie Wrap	58
Spicy Chicken Caesar Lettuce Cups	59
Protein-Packed Mediterranean Salad	59
Vibrant Veggie & Tuna Power Pack	60
Fresh & Zesty Turkey Wrap Supreme	60
DINNERS READY IN NO TIME	61
Zesty Lemon Chicken Express	62
Garlic Herb Salmon Surprise	62
Spicy Shrimp & Broccoli Blitz	63
Crispy Chicken Veggie Skillet	63
Basil Lime Beef Quick-Bake	64
Teriyaki Turkey Stir-Fry	64
Cauliflower Rice Chicken Bowl	65
Rapid Pesto Zoodle Chicken	65
Sizzling Steak & Pepper Medley	66
Mediterranean Chicken Fiesta	66
Homestyle Turkey Veggie Roast	67
Speedy Tofu & Veggie Curry	67
Flash-Fried Beef & Broccoli	68
Hearty Chicken Caesar Bake	68
Instant Avocado Lime Cod	69
Family Fiesta Shrimp Tacos	69
Express Eggplant Parmesan Bake	70
Chili Lime Chicken Fajitas	70
Wholesome Tofu & Spinach Stir-Fry	71
Lightning Beef Zoodle Bowl	71
STRESS-FREE SNACKS	72
Crunchy Almond Energy Bites	73
Zesty Tuna Cucumber Cups	73
Savory Veggie Hummus Cups	74
Spicy Turkey Jerky Bites	74
Cheddar Cauliflower Popper Bites	75
Nutty Seed Crunch Clusters	75
Protein-Packed Cottage Cheese Medallions	76
Avocado Lime Crisps	76
Smokin' Paprika Beef Jerky	77
Mini Egg Salad Lettuce Wraps	77
Quinoa Veggie Protein Balls	78
Chicken Caesar Snack Cups	78
Tangy Mediterranean Olive Bites	79
Kale & Parmesan Crisps	79
Tofu Satay Protein Nuggets	80
Spicy Shrimp Cocktail Cups	80
Greek Yogurt Berry Burst Cups	81
Zoodle Veggie Crunch Bites	81
Power Chia Pudding Poppers	82
Turbo Nutty Trail Mix	82
LIGHT DESSERTS	83
Velvety Dark Chocolate Avocado Mousse	84

Tropical Coconut Berry Bliss Parfait	84
Luscious Vanilla Protein Pudding Delight	85
Cinnamon-Spiced Apple Crisp Fantasy	85
Berry Burst Frozen Yogurt Jewels	86
Zesty Lemon Chia Radiance	86
Guiltless Almond Butter Fudge Indulgence	87
Minty Matcha Coconut Dream Bars	87
Fluffy Protein Pancake Sundae Surprise	88
Decadent Cocoa Protein Fudge Bliss	88
Peach Perfection Protein Custard	89
Refreshing Raspberry Lime Sorbet	89
Wholesome Pumpkin Spice Velvet Pudding	90
Crispy Baked Cinnamon-Kissed Pears	90
Choco-Banana Protein Ice Cream Delight	91
Vanilla Chia & Mixed Berry Symphony	91
Blueberry Almond Greek Yogurt Tart Temptation	92
No-Bake Peanut Butter Protein Bliss Bars	92
Strawberry Coconut Cream Dream Cups	93
Mocha Protein Mousse Magic	93
FAQ	**94**
Tips on Calorie and Macronutrient Tracking	95
FINAL ADVICE FOR LASTING CHANGE	**97**
EXTRA RESOURCES	**98**
Conversion Charts	98
Basic Grocery List	99
Seasonal Fruits & Vegetables Guide	101
30-Days Meal Plan	102
BONUS	**108**

WHO I AM

Hello there, I'm **Sarah Hollins**. I'm 36 years old, a mom of two bright and curious kids, and I live just outside of Austin, Texas. I'm not a doctor or a certified nutritionist, but I've spent a whole lot of time—years, really—researching and experimenting to find a healthy way of eating that actually fits into my busy life.

I still remember those long days when I'd try to juggle a demanding job, kids' activities, and family errands, only to realize at dinnertime that I had no plan for a quick, healthy meal. I'd rely on fast food or throw together something unbalanced just to fill everyone's stomachs. Over time, I noticed the weight creeping on, and the constant exhaustion didn't help my mood either. I was stuck in a frustrating cycle of telling myself, "I should eat better," but never feeling like I had enough time or energy to do so.

That's when I took a deep breath and decided to make a real change. I dove into research on high-protein, low-carb eating—reading, watching, asking questions in online groups—all in hopes of finding a method that was flexible, tasty, and actually doable for a mom with limited time. Slowly but surely, I started seeing results: I felt more energetic, I managed to shed the extra pounds, and my overall relationship with food became more positive.

I'm not here to say it was all sunshine and rainbows. There were days I'd come home from work totally beat, trying to wrangle two hungry kids while my stomach growled. But I stuck to simple principles—quick recipes that packed in the protein and left out the empty carbs—and discovered how to prep meals in advance so I wasn't scrambling every night. Bit by bit, cooking this way became second nature, and I realized something big: healthy eating doesn't have to be complicated, and it definitely doesn't have to be boring.

I want to share my story and my favorite tips with you because I've been on both sides—I know what it's like to feel overwhelmed and unsure of how to start. The recipes and strategies in this book are all about giving you back control in the kitchen and helping you reach a weight that makes you feel strong and confident. Everything I share comes from my personal journey and years of self-study. If you ever have medical questions, I encourage you to talk to a professional who can address your individual needs.

Most of all, I hope this book reminds you that you're not alone in wanting to eat better without sacrificing flavor or precious time. I believe wholeheartedly that with the right approach, you can take care of your health, enjoy amazing meals, and still have enough energy left over for the people and moments that matter most.

Let's do this together!

Sarah Hollins

WELCOME: WHY THIS BOOK CAN REALLY HELP YOU

Welcome to this journey toward a healthier, more vibrant version of yourself! You may be here because, like I once was, you're tired of feeling drained and disappointed by diets that promise quick fixes but don't offer real, lasting solutions. Or maybe you're simply looking for ideas to shake up your routine and keep your meals both satisfying and good for your body.

In the pages ahead, I'm going to share the practical tips, personal insights, and straight-to-the-point strategies that have helped me make peace with food and feel more energized day by day. I'm not a doctor or a certified nutritionist, just someone who's spent a lot of time experimenting, researching, and learning from my own ups and downs.

My hope is that you'll find something here—maybe a recipe, a new habit, or a spark of motivation—that makes all the difference in your life.

My Journey and Your Next Step

When I first started exploring new ways to eat and take care of myself, I was overwhelmed by all the conflicting information out there. One article would promise that carbs were the enemy, while another insisted it was all about cutting out fats. Then there were people swearing that only a raw or vegan lifestyle could possibly be healthy. Trying to figure out who was right and how it applied to my everyday life was enough to make me want to give up before I really began.

Looking back, what actually helped me move forward was embracing the idea that no one approach suits everyone. We're all built differently—our bodies respond in unique ways, and our schedules demand different levels of commitment. Once I realized that, I stopped searching for a "perfect" formula and started focusing on small, realistic changes. For me, that meant noticing how I felt after meals, paying attention to which foods made me feel sluggish, and experimenting with recipes I could actually see myself cooking on a busy weeknight.

Over time, I discovered how high-protein, low-carb meals gave me more consistent energy throughout the day. I could savor flavorful, satisfying dishes without feeling weighed down or deprived. Most importantly, it felt sustainable for me—I didn't have to reinvent my kitchen or my daily routine to make it work. That's when it clicked: maybe this way of eating wasn't a quick fix or a fad. Maybe it could be a real lifestyle shift, one that allowed me to enjoy food while treating my body with kindness.

Now I want to pass on what I've learned to you. Your next step is to find out how these ideas might fit into your own life. Take your time. Be curious. Figure out what kinds of meals, ingredients, and preparation methods excite you and fit your circumstances. Each chapter in this book is designed to help you do exactly that—so that instead of feeling restricted by your food choices, you can feel inspired and empowered.

Let's take this journey together.

How to Make the Most of These Pages

Think of this book as your personal roadmap—not a rigid set of rules, but a collection of practical tips, ideas, and experiences that you can adapt to fit your life. There's no "one-size-fits-all" solution when it comes to food and wellness, so feel free to pick and choose what resonates with you. Here's how I suggest you approach each chapter and get the maximum benefit:

Read with Curiosity
As you turn these pages, keep an open mind. If you come across a new concept or ingredient, take a moment to understand why it might be helpful or how it could simplify your routine. Maybe you'll love it, or maybe you'll realize it's not your thing—and that's totally okay. The goal is to discover what truly works for you.

Take It One Step at a Time
It can be tempting to dive headfirst into a new way of eating, but drastic changes often lead to burnout. Instead, try integrating small tweaks into your daily routine. For example, if you usually skip breakfast, consider adding a quick smoothie or scrambled eggs. If you're used to quick takeout lunches, maybe you'll

start by prepping just one homemade meal a week. These incremental shifts can make a big difference over time, and they're much easier to maintain than an all-or-nothing overhaul.

Use Each Chapter as a Building Block
You'll notice that the chapters are laid out in a progression—starting with foundational knowledge, moving through practical tips for saving time, and finally getting into the nuts and bolts of planning and cooking. Rather than skipping around, it might be helpful to read them in order, so you're gradually building up your toolbox of ideas and skills.
That said, if you're pressed for time and just need a fast lunch recipe, go straight to the lunch section—this book is here to serve you, not the other way around.

Adapt Recipes to Your Tastes and Needs
Each recipe you'll find later on can be tweaked. Don't be afraid to substitute ingredients, adjust seasonings, or alter cooking methods if it fits your schedule or personal preferences. Maybe you love spicy food, or you prefer lighter flavors—tailor the dishes to make them something you truly want to eat. If you have specific dietary concerns, like gluten intolerance or a dairy allergy, feel free to experiment with alternative ingredients.

Focus on Progress, Not Perfection
One of the biggest hurdles in any lifestyle change is feeling pressured to get it all right, all the time. The reality is that missteps happen. You'll have days when you're too busy to cook, times when you indulge in something sugary, or moments where old habits resurface. Let those moments be learning opportunities rather than failures. Reflect on what caused the slip, think about how you felt, and then move forward. Every small improvement you make is a step toward a healthier, more balanced life.

Stay Connected to Your "Why"
There's a reason you picked up this book—maybe you want more energy to keep up with your kids, or you're looking to feel more confident in your clothes, or perhaps you simply want to live a more balanced life. Whatever your motivation, remind yourself of it often. Write it down, set a phone reminder, or tell a friend who can keep you accountable.

This "why" will help guide your choices and keep you going when motivation dips.

Seek Professional Support When Needed
Remember, I'm not a doctor or nutritionist, and this book is based on personal experience and research I've done for myself. If you have specific concerns—such as medical conditions, food intolerances, or any questions about how certain foods interact with your body—please reach out to a qualified professional. They can give you personalized advice and help you tailor any plan to your unique situation.

In short, make these pages your own. Mark them up, take notes, highlight the parts that speak to you the most. The purpose of this book is to empower you, not to impose a rigid set of standards.

My hope is that by the end, you'll feel more confident in the kitchen, more at ease with your food choices, and more aware of how small, steady changes can lead to big transformations.

HIGH PROTEIN, LOW CARB: DISCOVER THE BENEFITS

Maybe you've heard whispers about high-protein, low-carb diets and are curious to find out what the buzz is all about. Or perhaps you've tried something similar in the past and want to give it another shot. Wherever you're coming from, this chapter is designed to give you a clear understanding of what "high-protein, low-carb" really means, and—more importantly—why it might help you feel more energetic, manage your weight, and develop a healthier relationship with food.

Over the years, I've learned that a high-protein, low-carb approach isn't just about numbers and ratios; it's about creating meals that genuinely fuel your body. When I first started exploring this way of eating, I noticed that focusing on protein and limiting processed carbs left me feeling fuller for longer, with fewer energy slumps throughout the day.
Suddenly, I wasn't grazing mindlessly on snacks every couple of hours, and I had the mental clarity to handle all the twists and turns of a busy schedule.

Of course, no single eating plan is universally perfect. But if you're willing to experiment and pay attention to how your body responds, you might just discover that a high-protein, low-carb diet can be flexible, tasty, and surprisingly simple to fit into everyday life. In the upcoming sections, we'll break down the basics—what these terms mean, how they affect your body, and the core ideas to remember when balancing your meals.

Think of this chapter as a friendly guide to get you started on your high-protein, low-carb journey. It's not about rigid meal plans or endless calculations; it's about understanding the fundamentals so you can confidently choose the foods that serve your well-being. Let's dive in.

What It Really Means

When I talk about a "high-protein, low-carb" way of eating, I'm referring to a simple shift in focus: choosing foods that are rich in protein—like lean meats, eggs, dairy, legumes, or plant-based proteins—and cutting back on foods high in refined carbohydrates and sugars. It doesn't mean you have to banish every carb from your plate, nor does it mean you should load up on bacon three times a day.

Instead, it's about finding a balance that helps you feel truly nourished, keeps your energy steady, and supports a healthier body composition over time.

Breaking It Down

High-Protein: Protein is often called the building block of life, and for good reason. It helps with muscle repair, balances hormones, and can even keep cravings in check by making you feel satisfied longer. Foods like chicken, fish, tofu, beans, and Greek yogurt pack a protein punch. You don't have to eat giant steaks daily—in fact, moderation is key—but aiming for a protein source at most meals can make a real difference in how you feel.

Low-Carb: Carbohydrates aren't the enemy. Fruits, vegetables, and whole grains can absolutely fit into a balanced meal plan. However, I discovered that cutting back on foods like white bread, pastries, and sugary snacks helped me avoid energy crashes and those sudden "I need to eat now" moments. Instead, I focus on complex carbs that come from whole grains or fiber-rich veggies.
These keep me feeling full and provide steady energy, rather than a quick spike followed by a slump.

A Flexible Approach

One of the misconceptions about high-protein, low-carb diets is that you have to meticulously track every gram of protein and carb. If you love numbers and spreadsheets, that's fine—but many people, including me, do just fine with a looser approach. By making sure each meal includes a solid protein source and by being mindful of where my carbs come from (often veggies, some fruits, and fewer refined grains), I find it easy to stay on track without obsessing over every detail.

Why It Works for Many People

Protein naturally promotes a feeling of fullness, which can help you keep cravings at bay and prevent overeating. Also, when your carbohydrate intake is moderated, you're less likely to experience drastic blood sugar spikes and crashes. This often translates to more consistent energy levels throughout the day. Over time, many people find that this style of eating helps support weight management, muscle maintenance, and a healthier relationship with food.

It's Not About Zero Carbs

I want to emphasize that "low-carb" is not the same as "no-carb." Our bodies do benefit from certain types of carbohydrates. Vegetables, fruits, and even some grains can be incredibly nutritious. The trick is to choose carbs that offer vitamins, minerals, and fiber—not just empty calories. Think of it as an invitation to eat a wider variety of colorful vegetables, to incorporate berries or other fruits when you crave something sweet, and to occasionally enjoy whole grains like brown rice or quinoa.

Ultimately, a high-protein, low-carb approach is about intentional eating. It's choosing foods that give you the most nutritional bang for your buck, keeping you satisfied and energized.

In the next sections, we'll explore exactly why focusing on protein can help you feel lighter and more energetic, and we'll unravel the basics of macronutrients so you can make informed decisions at every meal.

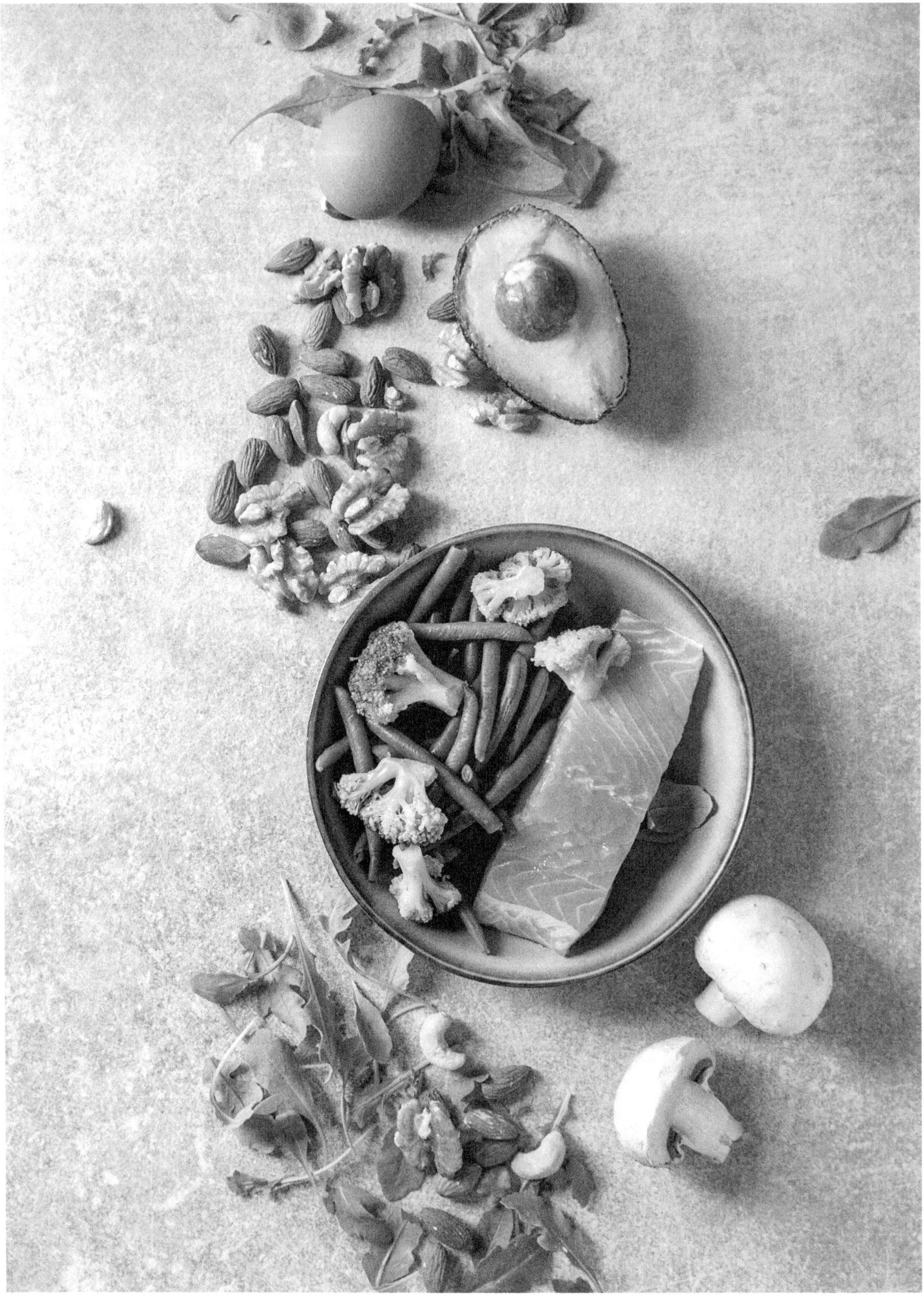

Why It Can Help You Feel Lighter and More Energetic

When I first started paying attention to how much protein I was eating versus how many carbs were filling up my plate, I noticed an immediate difference in how I felt throughout the day. Gone were the energy highs and lows that left me feeling jittery one moment and exhausted the next.
Instead, I experienced a steadier, more balanced sense of vitality.

Here's why high-protein, low-carb eating often has that effect:

1. **Steady Blood Sugar Levels**
   Picture your blood sugar like a roller coaster. When you consume a meal loaded with refined carbs or sugary snacks, you quickly ride up to a peak of energy—only to come crashing down soon after. This crash can leave you sleepy, moody, or craving more quick-fix carbs for another burst of energy. By focusing on protein and choosing carbs that are higher in fiber (like vegetables, fruits, or whole grains), you help your body maintain a more consistent blood sugar level. This translates to fewer spikes and crashes, which means more stable energy all day long.
2. **Longer-Lasting Fullness**
   Protein is known to be particularly satiating. Think about the last time you had a hearty chicken or tofu dish versus a meal centered on pasta or bread. Which one kept you satisfied longer? Chances are, the protein-heavy meal curbed your appetite for a good stretch of time. When you're not constantly battling hunger pangs or reaching for snacks, you can focus on the tasks and people that matter most, rather than being preoccupied with your next meal.
3. **Improved Muscle Support**
   Another reason many people feel lighter and more energetic on a high-protein diet is that protein helps build and maintain muscle mass. Muscle tissue burns more calories at rest than fat tissue, which can subtly boost your metabolism. Plus, having a bit more muscle can make everyday activities—like climbing the stairs or lugging groceries—feel easier and less tiring. Feeling physically stronger, even in small ways, often translates to feeling mentally and emotionally lighter too.
4. **Less Bloating and Discomfort**
   Many refined-carb foods—especially those loaded with added sugars or highly processed ingredients—can lead to bloating and digestive discomfort. By cutting back on these foods, you may notice that your belly feels flatter and more at ease. This simple reduction in discomfort can go a long way in making you feel light on your feet and more inclined to stay active.
5. **Balanced Nutrient Intake**
   A high-protein, low-carb lifestyle encourages you to be intentional about your food choices. Rather than mindlessly grabbing a bagel or ordering takeout, you're more likely to opt for lean proteins, nutrient-dense veggies, and healthy fats. Over time, this focus on whole foods—rich in vitamins, minerals, and fiber—can leave you feeling nourished from the inside out. When your body gets what it needs, it often responds with higher energy and improved overall well-being.
6. **Sustainable Energy for a Busy Lifestyle**
   If you're juggling work, family, personal projects, or all of the above, the last thing you need is a diet that leaves you constantly depleted. High-protein meals, paired with moderate, wholesome carbs, can provide that slow, steady release of energy that lets you power through a packed schedule. For me, that means fewer midday slumps and more mental clarity when I'm tackling my to-do list or spending quality time with my loved ones.
7. **A Boost in Confidence and Mindset**
   It's not just about the physical benefits. Feeling lighter and more energetic can also lift your mood and boost your confidence. When you're feeding your body well, you're sending yourself a message that you're worth investing in. That sense of self-care can ripple out into other areas of your life, encouraging you to move more, rest well, and take on new challenges with a positive mindset.

Remember, this isn't a magical cure-all; it's a starting point for a more mindful relationship with food. While many people experience these improvements by shifting toward a high-protein, low-carb approach, it's crucial to pay attention to your own body's signals. If something isn't working for you—if you feel overly tired, restricted, or uncomfortable—talk to a healthcare professional and consider making adjustments.

The key takeaway? By prioritizing protein and being thoughtful about the types of carbs you eat, you can often enjoy a level of energy and lightness that makes everyday life feel a bit more manageable—and a whole lot more enjoyable.

A Simple Explanation of Proteins, Carbs, and Fats

You've probably heard the term "**macronutrients**" (often shortened to "macros") if you've spent any time looking into nutrition or healthy eating. In the simplest terms, macronutrients are nutrients that our bodies require in larger quantities: proteins, carbohydrates, and fats. Each one plays a specific part in how we function every day, and understanding their roles can help you make better, more personalized choices when you prepare your meals.

Proteins: The Body's Building Blocks
- **Why They're Essential:**
  Proteins are involved in building and repairing muscles, organs, skin, and other tissues in the body.
  They also help produce enzymes and hormones—key messengers that regulate everything from digestion to mood.
  A protein-rich diet often helps you feel fuller for a longer period, making it less tempting to snack on junk food.
- **Where to Get Them:**
  Animal Sources: Chicken, turkey, fish (like salmon and tuna), lean cuts of beef or pork, eggs, dairy (such as Greek yogurt, cottage cheese, low-fat milk).
  Plant-Based Sources: Tofu, tempeh, beans, lentils, chickpeas, edamame, nuts, and seeds.
  Variety Counts: Even within animal or plant categories, rotating different protein sources ensures you get a broader spectrum of essential amino acids, vitamins, and minerals.
- **How Much Is Enough?**
  While there's no universal rule on how many grams of protein you "must" consume, many people aim for a source of protein at every meal—this could be a piece of chicken, a handful of nuts, or a cup of Greek yogurt, depending on your dietary choices and goals.

Carbohydrates: Your Body's Main Source of Energy
- **Why They're Essential:**
  Carbs convert into glucose, which your cells use for energy.
  They can be a quick-fuel option, especially when you need a burst of stamina—think of your morning workout or that midday slump at the office.
- **Different Types of Carbs:**
  Complex Carbs: Found in whole grains (brown rice, quinoa, oats), legumes (beans, lentils), and most vegetables. They contain fiber, which aids digestion and helps manage blood sugar levels more steadily.
  Simple Carbs: Found in foods like white bread, pastries, sugary cereals, and candy. These often cause rapid spikes in blood sugar followed by crashes, potentially leading to fatigue and cravings.
- **Choosing Quality Over Quantity:**
  You don't have to eliminate carbs entirely. Instead, focus on nutrient-dense options that provide vitamins, minerals, and fiber—like sweet potatoes, broccoli, or berries.
  If you do include simpler carbs (like white pasta or a sweet treat), consider pairing them with protein or healthy fats to slow digestion and avoid those energy crashes.

Fats: More Than Just an Energy Reserve
- **Why They're Essential:**
  Fats help with hormone regulation, brain function, and nutrient absorption (particularly for vitamins A, D, E, and K).
  They also add flavor and satiety to meals, helping you feel content after you eat.
- **Types of Fats:**
  Unsaturated Fats (Healthy Fats): Found in foods like avocados, olive oil, nuts (almonds, walnuts), seeds (chia, flax), and fatty fish (salmon, mackerel). These fats can support heart health and reduce inflammation.
  Saturated Fats: Present in butter, cheese, coconut oil, and fatty cuts of meat. While not all saturated fats are "bad," it's wise to monitor your intake and choose leaner options when possible.
  Trans Fats: Mostly found in processed foods and baked goods made with hydrogenated oils. These can negatively impact heart health, so it's best to limit or avoid them.
- **Balancing Fats in Your Diet:**
  Even with the good fats, moderation is key—fats are calorie-dense, so they can add up quickly. However, including a moderate portion of healthy fats in each meal can help keep hunger at bay and support overall well-being.

How Proteins, Carbs, and Fats Work Together

Instead of viewing these macros as isolated elements, it helps to see them as teammates working toward the common goal of fueling your body. When you eat a balanced meal—say, a lean protein source (chicken or tofu), paired with complex carbs (quinoa or sweet potato), plus a bit of healthy fat (avocado or olive oil)—you get:

- **Stable Energy:** Proteins and healthy fats help regulate how quickly carbs are digested, preventing dramatic blood sugar spikes or crashes.
- **Sustained Fullness:** The combination of protein and fiber (from veggies or whole grains) helps you stay satisfied longer, so you're not reaching for that cookie an hour later.
- **Essential Nutrient Coverage:** Each macro delivers different vitamins and minerals, ensuring you have a well-rounded intake that supports muscle, brain, and organ function.

Why This Matters in a High-Protein, Low-Carb Lifestyle

Aiming for a high-protein, low-carb approach means emphasizing proteins and re-evaluating the amount and type of carbs you eat, while not neglecting healthy fats. It does not necessarily mean cutting carbs out entirely or fearing fats. Instead, you'll be more intentional about where your carbs come from (opting for vegetables, legumes, and moderate amounts of whole grains) and how much you include.

You'll still get plenty of vitamins, minerals, and fiber by focusing on whole, nutrient-rich foods.
You can enjoy a steady flow of energy, rather than the peaks and valleys that sometimes accompany a high-sugar or heavily processed diet.

Protein becomes the star player, ensuring muscle maintenance, satiety, and a feeling of sustained fullness that helps you avoid overindulging on less nutritious fare.

Key Takeaways

Proteins are essential for building and repairing your body's cells, and they help you stay full and satisfied.
Carbs come in different forms—stick to complex, nutrient-dense ones for steady energy and skip or limit refined sugars.
Fats are crucial for hormone regulation, brain function, and nutrient absorption; focus on healthy sources like avocados, nuts, and olive oil.

Balance Is Your Friend:
Combine these macronutrients in a way that supports your energy needs, tastes good to you, and fits your lifestyle.

By understanding the roles these macronutrients play, you'll be more confident in planning meals that truly nourish you. Up next, we'll talk about how to balance these nutrients in a way that doesn't feel restrictive or complicated—because healthy eating should be about enjoyment and well-being, not endless rules.

Balancing Nutrients Without Stress

It's one thing to know about proteins, carbs, and fats, but it's another thing entirely to put them together in a way that feels sustainable and not at all overwhelming. One of the biggest lessons I've learned on my journey is that balance doesn't have to be complicated—or stressful. By keeping a few guiding principles in mind, you can build meals that nourish your body and still delight your taste buds.

1. **Use Your Plate as a Visual Guide**
   One of the simplest ways to balance your meals is to imagine your plate divided into sections:
   Half for Non-Starchy Vegetables: Think broccoli, leafy greens, zucchini, peppers, or cauliflower. These deliver essential vitamins and minerals and are generally lower in carbs.
   A Quarter for Protein: Whether it's chicken, fish, tofu, or lentils, protein helps keep you satisfied while supporting muscle maintenance.
   A Quarter for Healthy Carbs or Fats: This could be a serving of quinoa, brown rice, or sweet potato if you want more carbs, or an avocado slice, nuts, or seeds if you're leaning toward healthy fats. Of course, if you prefer, you can include a bit of both—just be mindful of portions. Using this visual approach can simplify your meal planning without requiring complex calculations or measuring cups for every bite.
2. **Choose Quality Over Quantity**
   Rather than worrying about the exact grams of each macronutrient, focus on quality. Carbs from white bread and sugary snacks are less beneficial than carbs from vegetables, fruits, or

whole grains. The same goes for protein—opting for a lean chicken breast, fish, or a well-balanced plant-based protein usually offers more nutritional value than processed, high-sodium deli meats.

When it comes to fats, unsaturated sources like olive oil, avocados, nuts, and seeds tend to benefit your heart and overall health more than heavy fried foods or sweets high in trans fats. By prioritizing nutrient-dense whole foods, you naturally wind up with a plate that's higher in protein and healthy fats, and lower in simple carbs.

3. **Embrace Flexibility and Experimentation**
   There's no need to feel boxed in by rigid rules. If you're craving a bit of pasta or a piece of fresh bread, it doesn't have to be off-limits—just balance it out with a protein source and some colorful veggies. You might discover that you can still enjoy certain high-carb foods in moderation without derailing your goals.

   Experiment with new ingredients or cooking styles, and pay attention to how you feel afterward. For instance, if you try a dish that's heavier in carbs, note whether you feel energized or sluggish. If you lean on a meal that's high in protein and healthy fats, do you stay full longer? Over time, you'll pinpoint the sweet spot where you feel your best.

4. **Plan Ahead When You Can**
   When life gets busy—and it will—having a basic plan can prevent last-minute decisions that might not align with your goals. It doesn't mean you need to spend hours in the kitchen. Simple tasks like cooking extra chicken or tofu to use in salads throughout the week can be a huge time-saver. Slicing up vegetables in advance or portioning out healthy snack options also makes balanced eating more convenient.

   Planning ahead helps you avoid that frantic "What's for dinner?" panic. Instead, you'll have components ready to mix and match—protein, veggies, healthy carbs, and fats—to create quick, nourishing meals.

5. **Listen to Your Body's Signals**
   Even with the best-laid plans, your appetite, energy level, and cravings can vary day by day. Learning to trust your body is a skill that takes practice but can drastically reduce stress around food. If you're full before finishing your plate, don't force yourself to keep eating. Conversely, if you feel genuinely hungry after a balanced meal, it might be time to adjust portion sizes or include more of one macronutrient.

   Remember that feeling good is the ultimate goal. If you notice consistent bloating, fatigue, or discomfort, it might be your body's way of telling you that something in your meals isn't quite right. Experiment with small adjustments—maybe it's reducing dairy, swapping one carb source for another, or adding more leafy greens—and see if it makes a difference.

6. **Don't Sweat the Occasional Indulgence**
   Balance also means leaving room for life's simple pleasures. Whether it's a slice of birthday cake or a spontaneous ice cream run on a hot summer day, occasional treats can still fit into a high-protein, low-carb approach. Give yourself permission to enjoy these moments and then move on, returning to the principles that keep you feeling your best. Guilt rarely helps anyone—it's the steady, overall pattern of your eating habits that truly matters in the long run.

Putting It All Together

Balancing nutrients doesn't have to revolve around strict rules or complicated math. By visualizing your plate, choosing high-quality foods, staying flexible, and trusting your body's cues, you'll set yourself up for a lifestyle that supports both your health and your happiness. The goal isn't perfection—it's finding a rhythm that allows you to enjoy meals, feel energized, and handle whatever life throws your way.

In the chapters ahead, you'll discover practical tips for saving time, meal prepping, and crafting delicious recipes that can be adapted to your own tastes. Stick with these core principles, and you'll find that high-protein, low-carb eating can fit seamlessly into your busy life without the stress that often comes with diet changes. Remember, you're building a sustainable foundation—one balanced meal at a time.

SAVE TIME WITHOUT GIVING UP FLAVOR

Welcome to a chapter designed especially for those of us who lead busy lives but refuse to compromise on taste or nutrition. I know how overwhelming it can be to juggle work, family, and everyday errands, all while trying to put together a healthy meal. There was a time when I felt like I had no minutes to spare, and the idea of cooking a nutritious dinner seemed impossible.

In this section, I'll share practical tips and tricks that have transformed my approach to meal planning and cooking. You'll learn how to shop smart, choose the right kitchen tools, and prepare ingredients in advance—all while keeping your meals delicious and satisfying. Whether you're a seasoned multitasker or just beginning to explore the world of time-saving cooking, this chapter is here to help you reclaim your evenings and enjoy flavorful, healthy dishes without feeling rushed.

Let's dive in and discover how you can save time in the kitchen while still creating meals that nourish both your body and your taste buds.

Smart Grocery Shopping

Grocery shopping can feel overwhelming, especially on hectic days when you're juggling work, family, and countless other responsibilities. I remember one Tuesday when everything seemed to be happening at once—my kids were buzzing with excitement for a last-minute school field trip, my work emails were piling up, and I was determined not to end the day with a rushed, unhealthy dinner. That day, I decided to try a new strategy: I planned my meals for the week and headed to the store with a detailed list in hand.

- **Plan Your Meals First:**
  Before stepping into the store, I sat down with a cup of coffee and mapped out a simple menu for the week. I chose recipes that were quick, flavorful, and aligned with my high-protein, low-carb goals—dishes like grilled chicken with a colorful salad, a veggie-packed stir-fry with tofu, and a hearty bean soup. This planning not only gave me a clear idea of what to buy but also

helped me feel confident that I was setting up my family for nutritious, satisfying meals.

- **Make a Detailed List:**
Armed with my menu, I wrote down every ingredient I would need, grouping items by category. On that Tuesday, my list included lean chicken breasts, fresh spinach, bell peppers, a variety of nuts, and even a few unexpected items like a jar of homemade salsa to add a burst of flavor. Having this organized list transformed my shopping trip from a chaotic wander through endless aisles into a focused mission.
- **Check Your Pantry:**
I always make it a point to quickly scan my pantry before shopping. I recalled that I already had a bag of quinoa and some spices left over from previous meals. This simple step not only saved money but also reduced food waste—plus, it gave me a sense of satisfaction knowing I was making the most of what I already had.
- **Embrace Seasonal and Local Produce:**
On that trip, I discovered a beautiful basket of seasonal strawberries at the local produce section. They were so vibrant and sweet, a perfect, natural treat that fit right into my vision of a balanced diet. I've learned that seasonal produce is often more flavorful and affordable, and it never fails to inspire new recipe ideas.
- **Read Labels and Choose Wisely:**
Another lesson came from a past experience when I almost fell for a "healthy" cereal that, upon closer inspection, was loaded with hidden sugars. Now, I always take a moment to check labels. It's a habit that not only prevents unwanted surprises but also reinforces my commitment to choosing real, whole foods.
- **Bulk Buying and Smart Substitutions:**
There was a time I bought a large pack of nuts at a bulk store, thinking I'd use them all. However, I ended up with more than I could consume before they went stale. Now, I'm more mindful of buying in bulk only when I'm certain I can use the ingredients in time, and I keep a mental list of smart substitutes—for example, swapping out one type of protein for another if my favorite isn't available.
- **Stick to the Perimeter:**
I've found that most of the healthiest options are right at the store's perimeter—fresh fruits, vegetables, dairy, and meats. Focusing on this area helped me avoid the processed foods that often tempt me down the middle aisles. It's a strategy that's become second nature over the years and really simplifies the decision-making process.
- **Avoid Shopping When Hungry:**
Finally, I've learned the hard way that grocery shopping on an empty stomach is a recipe for unnecessary purchases. I always have a small, healthy snack before I head out, whether it's an apple or a handful of almonds. This simple trick helps me keep cravings in check and ensures I stick to my list.

By embracing these smart shopping strategies, I've turned a potentially stressful errand into an empowering start to my week. A well-planned, organized shopping trip not only fills your pantry with the right ingredients but also sets the stage for a week of easy, delicious, and nourishing meals.

Trust me, those little adjustments in how you shop can make a huge difference in your overall journey to healthier eating.

Handy Tools and Quick Cooking Methods

One of the biggest game-changers in my kitchen has been discovering the right tools and techniques to speed up cooking without sacrificing flavor. When I first started juggling a busy schedule with work and family, I knew I needed to streamline my time in the kitchen. Over the years, I've assembled a collection of gadgets and honed a few quick-cooking methods that have made meal preparation both efficient and enjoyable.

Essential Kitchen Tools

- **Instant Pot/Pressure Cooker:**
This appliance has truly revolutionized the way I cook. With an Instant Pot, I can prepare a tender stew or perfectly steamed vegetables in a fraction of the time it would take on the stovetop. I remember the first time I used it—I was skeptical about pressure cooking, but when I pulled out a delicious, fall-off-the-bone chicken dish after just 20 minutes, I was hooked.
- **Air Fryer:**
If you love that crispy texture without the extra oil, the air fryer is a must-have. It's perfect for quickly crisping up vegetables, making protein like chicken tenders healthier, or even reheating

leftovers while keeping them delightfully crunchy. My kids absolutely love the air-fried fries I whip up on busy evenings.
- **Food Processor or Blender:**
A good food processor can chop vegetables in seconds, make delicious pesto, or even help prepare dough for quick flatbreads. For me, blending has become essential when I'm in the mood for a protein-packed smoothie or a quick sauce to dress up a salad. These tools cut down prep time dramatically and allow you to experiment with new recipes without a fuss.
- **Non-Stick Pans and Sheet Pans:**
High-quality non-stick pans save me a ton of time and energy—they heat quickly, require less oil, and are easy to clean. Similarly, sheet pans are fantastic for making one-pan meals. I often toss together a medley of vegetables with a lean protein, season generously, and roast everything together in a preheated oven for a no-hassle, nutrient-packed dinner.

Quick Cooking Methods

- **Stir-Frying:**
Stir-frying is one of my go-to methods for preparing a speedy yet flavorful meal. All you need is a hot pan or wok, a bit of oil, and your favorite vegetables and protein. Within minutes, you have a vibrant dish that's full of texture and taste. I love experimenting with different sauces—like a light teriyaki or a spicy garlic mix—that elevate the simple ingredients to something truly special.
- **Batch Cooking:**
Not a cooking method per se, but a strategy that saves time in the long run. I often spend a few hours on the weekend preparing large batches of grilled chicken, roasted veggies, or quinoa. Then, during the week, I can mix and match these pre-cooked components to create a variety of meals in minutes. This approach not only simplifies cooking but also helps me maintain my high-protein, low-carb lifestyle without scrambling for ingredients every day.
- **Microwave Techniques:**
While the microwave might seem like a shortcut for reheating leftovers, it can be a powerful tool for quick cooking too. I use it to steam vegetables, melt healthy fats like olive oil for a quick drizzle over salads, or even "bake" a mug omelet when I'm in a hurry. It's all about using the appliance creatively to suit your nutritional needs.
- **One-Pot or One-Pan Meals:**
The fewer pots you have to wash, the better! One-pot meals—like a hearty stew or a one-pan roasted dinner—are ideal for busy days. They allow you to combine protein, veggies, and healthy carbs all in one go, reducing not only cooking time but also clean-up time afterward. I often rely on these meals during particularly hectic weeks when every minute counts.

Bringing It All Together

Having the right tools and mastering quick cooking methods has transformed my approach to meal preparation. It's not about cutting corners or sacrificing flavor; it's about being smart with your time and using technology and techniques that empower you in the kitchen. Whether you're a seasoned cook or just starting out, these strategies can help you create delicious, nutritious meals—even on the busiest days.

Remember, the goal is to make cooking an enjoyable, stress-free part of your day. Experiment with these tools and methods until you find what works best for you, and soon enough, you'll discover that preparing a high-protein, low-carb meal can be both fast and incredibly satisfying.

Meal Prepping Made Easy

Meal prepping is one of those simple yet powerful strategies that can transform your week from chaotic to calm. I remember the days when every evening felt like a frantic scramble to throw together dinner after a long, exhausting day.

Then I discovered that spending just a couple of hours on the weekend planning and preparing my meals could save me so much time—and stress—during the busy weekdays.

Start Small and Keep It Simple
For me, meal prepping isn't about preparing elaborate dishes that require hours in the kitchen. It's about planning a few key components that can be mixed and matched throughout the week. For example, I might grill a batch of chicken breasts, roast a tray of mixed vegetables, and cook a pot of quinoa. Then, on any given day, I can quickly assemble a balanced plate by combining these prepped ingredients with a simple dressing or sauce.

Invest in Good Containers
A game-changer in my meal prepping journey was investing in quality, airtight containers. Not only do they keep my food fresh, but they also help with portion control. I like to label each container with the date and the meal it's intended for. This little habit makes it easy to grab what I need on hectic mornings or during a busy lunch break at work.

Plan Ahead with a Menu
Planning your menu for the week might sound like extra work, but it really pays off. I take a few minutes each Sunday to jot down a simple plan—something flexible enough to allow for a little spontaneity but structured enough to keep me on track. Whether it's a hearty salad for lunch or a stir-fry for dinner, knowing what you're aiming for in advance means fewer last-minute decisions and less temptation to reach for unhealthy convenience foods.

Keep a Balance of Flavors and Textures
One of my biggest worries when I first started meal prepping was that my food would become boring or repetitive. To combat this, I mix up the flavors and textures by preparing versatile components. A batch of roasted vegetables can be enjoyed warm with a sprinkle of Parmesan, or chilled in a salad with a tangy vinaigrette. The grilled chicken can be sliced and tossed into a wrap or served over a bed of greens. By keeping things varied, you'll always look forward to your next meal.

Use Freezer-Friendly Recipes
Sometimes, even with meal prepping, unexpected events can throw off your plan. That's why I love having a few freezer-friendly meals on hand. I often make a big pot of soup or stew that freezes beautifully, so on days when I'm really pressed for time, I can simply reheat a nourishing bowl of goodness without any fuss.

Celebrate Small Wins
Every time I pull out my neatly labeled containers from the fridge and enjoy a stress-free, delicious meal, I feel a little victory. Meal prepping isn't about perfection—it's about making your life easier and more manageable. Even if things don't go exactly as planned, having a few ready-to-eat options is far better than scrambling to figure out dinner at the last minute.

The Impact on Your Life
Since incorporating meal prepping into my routine, I've noticed a significant improvement not only in my energy levels but also in my overall well-being. I feel less rushed, more in control, and more confident that I'm fueling my body with wholesome, balanced meals. Plus, the extra time saved allows me to enjoy a quiet cup of coffee in the morning or a peaceful moment with my family in the evening.

Meal prepping made easy is all about simplicity, planning, and flexibility. Start small, experiment with different recipes, and soon you'll find a system that works perfectly for you.

This approach not only supports your high-protein, low-carb lifestyle but also frees up your time so you can focus on what truly matters in your day.

Small Steps to Stay Motivated Day by Day

Staying motivated isn't about making huge changes overnight—it's about taking small, manageable steps every day that build into lasting habits. I remember a day not too long ago when I felt completely overwhelmed. I had just come home from a long, stressful day at work and was exhausted from chasing after my kids all afternoon.

I found myself staring into the fridge, feeling defeated and tempted to order fast food—a quick, easy way out that, I knew, wouldn't support my long-term goals.

That evening, I gave in. I ordered a meal that wasn't aligned with my high-protein, low-carb plan, and afterwards, I felt disappointed and guilty. But rather than letting that setback define me, I decided to use it as a learning experience. I reminded myself that one slip-up doesn't erase all the progress I've made.

Instead, I focused on one small promise: tomorrow, I would take one simple, healthy step.

Over time, these small victories have accumulated. I began keeping a journal where I noted every healthy choice—whether it was swapping a sugary snack for a piece of fruit, taking a brisk 10-minute walk during a busy day, or planning my meals in advance.

Reading back on these little wins reminded me that progress isn't about perfection—it's about persistence.

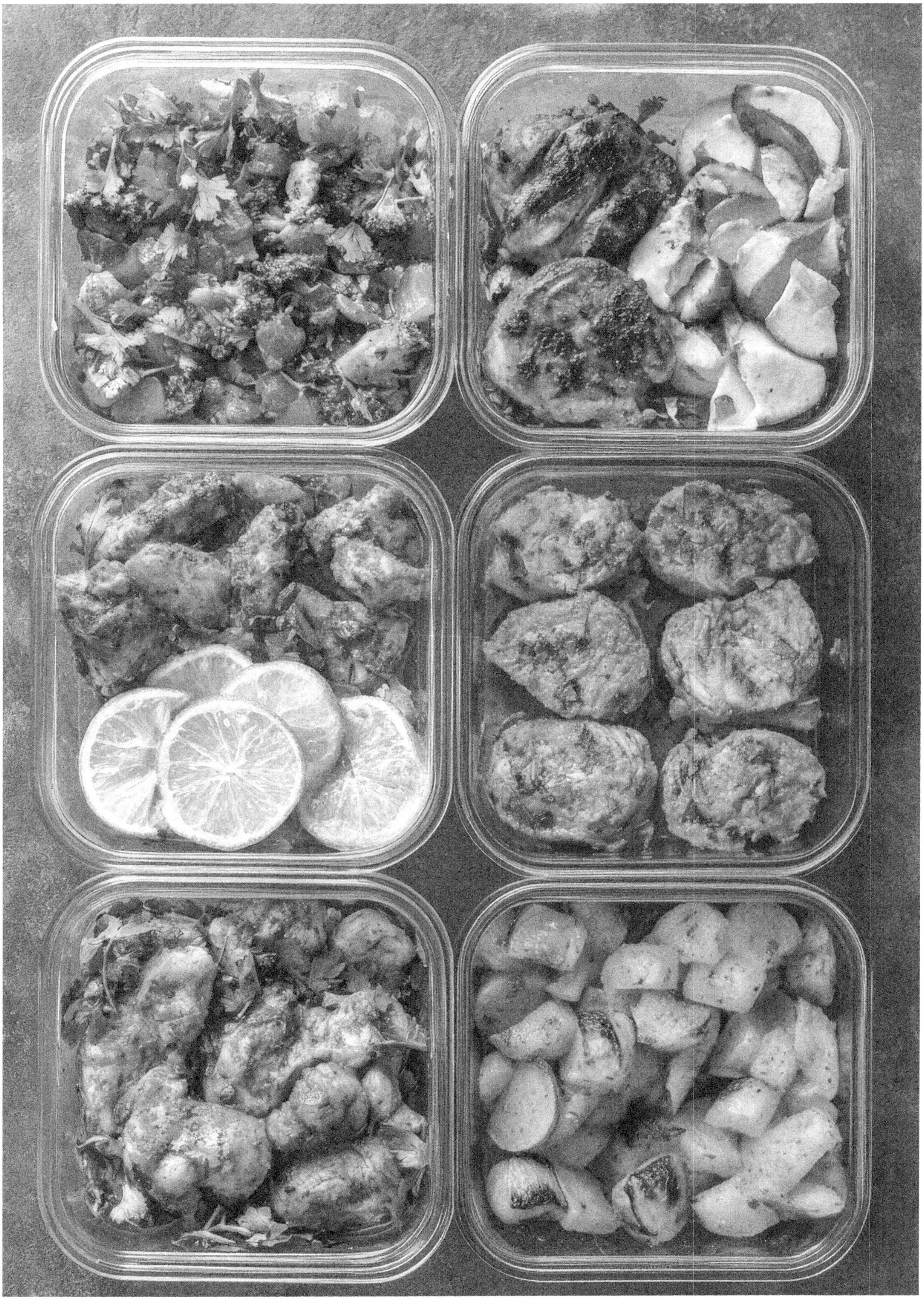

Practical Tips to Keep You Moving Forward:

- **Start with One Change:**
  Choose a small goal to focus on each week. For instance, commit to having a protein-rich breakfast every morning. Once that becomes a habit, add another goal, like preparing a healthy lunch for work. This gradual approach prevents feeling overwhelmed.
- **Keep a Daily Journal:**
  Write down one healthy choice you made each day. It could be as simple as opting for a salad over fries or taking a short walk. When you look back, you'll see a collection of positive actions that build up your motivation.
- **Set Reminders:**
  Use your phone or sticky notes to remind you of your goals. A gentle reminder to drink water, prepare your lunch, or take a few moments to stretch can keep you on track, even on busy days.
- **Celebrate Your Wins:**
  Recognize and reward yourself for sticking to your plan, even if it's just a small victory. It might be something simple like watching an episode of your favorite show guilt-free or enjoying a quiet moment with a good book. These little rewards can reinforce your commitment to a healthier lifestyle.
- **Plan for Setbacks:**
  Understand that there will be days when things don't go as planned. When you feel tempted to stray, plan a quick strategy—a healthy snack you can prepare in advance or a few minutes of deep breathing to refocus your energy. This proactive approach can help you bounce back quickly from a setback.
- **Lean on Your Support Network:**
  Share your goals and small victories with a friend or family member. Sometimes, a quick text exchange or a supportive conversation can make all the difference on a tough day. If you have an online group or community, consider sharing your experiences there as well.

Every healthy choice, no matter how small, is a step in the right direction. Remember, the journey is about progress, not perfection. By taking one small step at a time and using practical strategies to keep you on track, you can build the momentum that leads to lasting, positive change.

Keep moving forward—you've got this!

BEFORE YOU START COOKING: WHAT YOU NEED TO KNOW

Before you dive into creating quick, nutritious meals, it's important to set yourself up for success in the kitchen. This chapter is all about laying a solid foundation so that cooking feels more like a fun, creative activity rather than a stressful chore.

I want to share some of the key insights and practical tips that have helped me build confidence in the kitchen—especially on those hectic days when time is short. Here, you'll learn how to organize your workspace, make sense of ingredient labels, and break down recipes into manageable steps.

You'll also discover simple ways to tweak a dish to match your personal taste or dietary needs without feeling overwhelmed.

Imagine starting your day with a clear plan: knowing exactly where your tools are, having a few staple ingredients on hand, and understanding the basics of the recipes you're about to try. Whether it's setting up your counter with all your cutting boards, knives, and measuring cups arranged neatly, or reviewing a recipe step-by-step before you begin, these small habits make a big difference.

I'll also explain how to interpret recipe instructions, adjust portions, and even substitute ingredients when needed. For instance, if a recipe calls for a particular vegetable you can't find, I'll share some ideas on what you can use instead, ensuring that you always have options.

The goal is to help you feel empowered and adaptable in the kitchen—ready to take on any recipe with a clear plan in mind.

By the end of this chapter, you'll have a toolkit of essential strategies to help you navigate the cooking process smoothly. Whether you're a busy parent, a working professional, or someone who's just starting to explore healthy cooking, these tips will make your time in the kitchen enjoyable and stress-free.

Let's take this first step together toward creating meals that are as satisfying to prepare as they are to eat.

What You'll Find in the Next Pages

In this section, I want to give you a clear picture of what lies ahead in this book and how each part is designed to help you transform your cooking and eating habits. As you turn each page, you'll discover a blend of practical tips, personal stories, and step-by-step guidance that makes healthy, high-protein, low-carb cooking both approachable and enjoyable.

Here's a snapshot of what you can expect:

- **Easy-to-Follow Guidance:**
  You'll find clear explanations of the basics—from understanding ingredient labels to setting up your workspace. I've broken everything down into simple, manageable steps, so you never feel overwhelmed by a recipe or technique.
- **Personal Insights and Real-Life Examples:**
  Throughout the book, I share my own experiences in the kitchen—the successes, the slip-ups, and the lessons learned along the way. For example, I'll tell you about the time I scrambled to prepare a dinner for a busy evening and how a little prep work made all the difference. These stories aren't just anecdotes; they're practical insights designed to inspire and reassure you that you're not alone on this journey.
- **Adaptable Strategies:**
  Whether you're a seasoned cook or just starting out, you'll find strategies that can be tailored to fit your lifestyle. From meal prepping tips to quick-cooking methods, the ideas here are flexible enough to work with your schedule and your personal tastes. I want you to feel empowered to experiment and make each recipe your own.
- **Practical Tips and Tricks:**
  Expect plenty of time-saving hacks, like how to streamline your grocery shopping or use simple kitchen tools effectively. You'll also learn how to substitute ingredients when something isn't available, ensuring that you always have options without feeling stuck.
- **Step-by-Step Processes:**
  Each chapter is structured in a way that builds your confidence gradually. Starting with foundational advice, we move on to more detailed cooking methods and finally into the recipes themselves. This progression helps you build a solid skill set and a better understanding of how to mix and match nutrients for balanced, satisfying meals.
- **Encouragement and Motivation:**
  Healthy eating isn't just about the food—it's about making choices that support your overall well-being. You'll find sections dedicated to small steps to stay motivated and tips on how to celebrate your progress, no matter how small. I want you to feel excited about the journey, knowing that every healthy choice you make is a step toward a better, more energetic you.

By the time you finish these pages, you'll have a practical toolkit for transforming your kitchen routine. You'll understand not only how to cook quick, nutritious meals but also how to adapt them to your life. Whether you're looking to save time, feel more energized, or simply enjoy your food more, this book is designed to be your supportive guide every step of the way.

So, take a deep breath and get ready to dive in. The next pages are packed with insights, inspiration, and actionable tips that will make healthy cooking an exciting part of your day.

Let's embark on this journey together, one page at a time.

Reading Ingredients and Following Instructions with Ease

One of the secrets to stress-free cooking is truly understanding what goes into your recipes and feeling confident about following the instructions step by step. Over time, I've learned that mastering this skill not only saves time but also opens up a world of creative possibilities in the kitchen.

Let me share some detailed insights on how to read ingredients and follow recipe instructions with ease.

Understanding the Ingredient List
Every recipe begins with an ingredient list, which might seem intimidating at first if you're not familiar with some of the terms. Here's how to break it down:

- **Know Your Terms:**
  Familiarize yourself with common cooking terms and measurements. For example, "minced garlic"

simply means garlic that has been finely chopped, and "room temperature" indicates that the ingredient should not be too cold or hot before mixing into a recipe. A quick search or a handy glossary in your cookbook can be invaluable.

- **Identify Key Ingredients:**
  Look at the list and pinpoint the core components that define the dish. Is it the protein that's central, or perhaps a particular spice blend that gives the recipe its character? Understanding which ingredients are essential helps you decide if you need to purchase high-quality versions or if you have acceptable substitutes on hand.
- **Spot the Extras:**
  Many recipes include additional ingredients for flavor or texture—like herbs, spices, or garnishes. These extras can often be adjusted to suit your taste or what's available in your pantry without drastically changing the outcome of the dish.

Interpreting Recipe Instructions

Recipes can sometimes feel like a puzzle, especially if the instructions are packed with details. Here are some strategies to help you follow along smoothly:

- **Read Through the Entire Recipe First:**
  Before you start cooking, take a few minutes to read the recipe from start to finish. This gives you a clear idea of the process and helps you mentally prepare for each step. It also highlights any techniques you might need to review or ingredients you need to prep in advance.
- **Break Down the Steps:**
  If a recipe has multiple parts—like a marinade, a sauce, and the main dish—break it down into individual sections. You might even consider writing a quick outline or checklist on a piece of paper to ensure you don't miss a step.
- **Visualize the Process:**
  As you read, try to imagine what each step looks like. For instance, if the recipe says "sauté the onions until they are translucent," picture the texture and color you're aiming for. This mental rehearsal can make the actual cooking process feel much more familiar.
- **Ask Questions:**
  If you come across an instruction that isn't clear, don't hesitate to look up a quick video tutorial online or consult a cooking guide. There's a wealth of resources out there that can provide a visual demonstration of a tricky technique.

Practical Tips for a Smooth Cooking Experience

I've had my fair share of moments when I jumped into a recipe only to realize halfway through that I wasn't quite sure what "julienne" meant, or that I'd misread a measurement. Here are some practical tips that have helped me avoid those pitfalls:

- **Prep and Organize:**
  Before turning on any heat, gather and measure all your ingredients. This "mise en place" (everything in its place) not only makes the process less chaotic but also allows you to spot any items you might need to substitute.
- **Keep a Cheat Sheet:**
  Create a personal reference list of common terms, measurements, and techniques. Over time, you'll build up your own mini-guide that makes reading recipes much easier. I often keep a small notebook or digital document with notes on substitutions, timing, and even reminders about my favorite methods.
- **Take Your Time:**
  Especially when you're just starting out, give yourself permission to work slowly and carefully. There's no rush—cooking is meant to be a pleasurable experience. The more you practice, the more intuitive reading and following recipes will become.
- **Reflect on Past Experiences:**
  Think back to times when you successfully cooked a meal. What made it work? Often, it's because you took the time to carefully read through the recipe and prepared everything in advance. Use those positive experiences as a reminder that you can handle more complicated recipes with a little extra attention.

It's All About Enjoyment, Not Perfection

I want to emphasize that the aim of mastering these skills isn't to turn you into a Michelin-starred chef overnight. The goal here is much simpler: to make the act of cooking—and even eating—an enjoyable, satisfying, and ultimately rewarding experience.

These tips are meant to help you create meals that are both healthy and delicious, so you can nurture your body while also improving your relationship with food. It's about making the kitchen a place where creativity flows and every dish you prepare feels like a small win.

Rather than stressing over every measurement or

technique, remember that the beauty of cooking lies in its flexibility. Experiment, have fun, and allow yourself the freedom to adjust recipes to suit your tastes and lifestyle. The real reward is discovering that healthy, high-protein, low-carb meals can be both straightforward and flavorful—transforming your daily routine into a delightful journey of nourishment and joy.

By taking the time to understand and apply these simple strategies, you'll build confidence in the kitchen, and soon enough, following recipes will feel like second nature.

Enjoy the process, savor the learning, and most importantly, have fun as you make every meal a celebration of healthy eating.

Adapting Recipes to Your Needs

One of the most empowering parts of cooking is learning how to make a recipe truly your own. Over time, I discovered that recipes aren't strict blueprints set in stone—they're flexible guidelines that you can adjust to suit your tastes, dietary needs, or even what you have on hand.

This approach not only makes cooking more accessible but also turns every meal into a creative, personalized experience.

Understanding Your Own Preferences
Before you start tweaking a recipe, take a moment to reflect on what you enjoy. Do you love a little extra spice, or do you prefer milder flavors? Perhaps you have dietary restrictions—maybe you're lactose intolerant or need to avoid gluten. Knowing what works for you makes it easier to see where adjustments are needed.

For example, if you're not a fan of a particular vegetable in a stir-fry, consider swapping it for another that offers a similar texture or nutritional benefit.

A Personal Story of Adaptation
I remember a time when I was excited to try a new high-protein chicken curry recipe. The original version called for coconut milk and a specific blend of spices that, frankly, didn't match my taste. I found the coconut flavor too strong and the spice mix a bit overpowering. Instead of scrapping the recipe altogether, I made a few adjustments. I swapped the coconut milk for a lighter almond milk and reduced some of the spicier elements, adding a pinch of cinnamon to balance the flavors. The result was a dish that still carried the spirit of the original recipe but was perfectly tailored to my palate. That small tweak transformed what could have been a disappointing meal into one of my new favorites.

Practical Tips for Adaptation

1. **Substitute Thoughtfully:**
   If an ingredient isn't available or doesn't suit your taste, look for a substitute that maintains the nutritional balance. For example, if a recipe calls for heavy cream and you're looking for a lighter option, try Greek yogurt or a plant-based alternative. Experimenting with swaps can lead you to discover new flavor combinations that you might not have considered otherwise.
2. **Adjust Seasonings Gradually:**
   When it comes to herbs and spices, start with a smaller amount than what the recipe suggests. You can always add more as you taste along the way. This gradual approach ensures you don't accidentally overpower the dish and helps you find that sweet spot where all the flavors harmonize.
3. **Modify Cooking Methods:**
   Sometimes, adapting a recipe isn't just about changing ingredients. You might also consider different cooking methods. If you're short on time, try a quick sauté instead of a slow simmer. Or if you prefer a crispier texture, a brief stint in the air fryer might do the trick. Adjusting cooking techniques can make the recipe fit better into your lifestyle without compromising on taste or nutrition.
4. **Embrace Flexibility:**
   Remember that recipes are starting points. Don't be afraid to experiment and make adjustments based on what's available in your kitchen or your current mood. Over time, these adaptations will become second nature, and you'll start to develop your own signature touches that make each dish uniquely yours.

The Bigger Picture

Adapting recipes is about more than just personal taste—it's a step toward building a healthier relationship with food. By tailoring dishes to meet

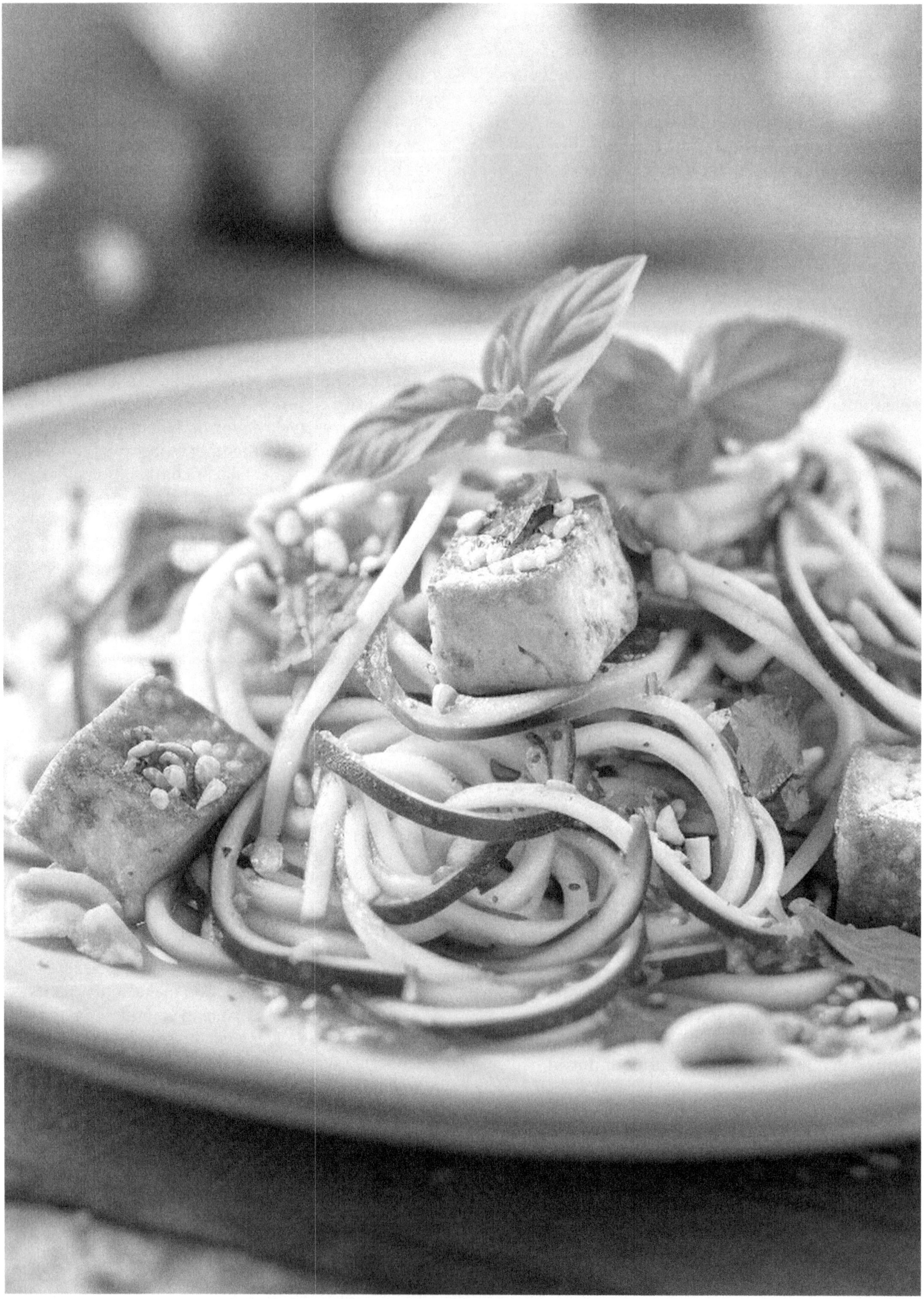

your needs, you're not only ensuring that every meal is enjoyable but also reinforcing the idea that healthy eating is flexible and sustainable. It's an opportunity to celebrate your individuality in the kitchen, making each meal a small act of self-care.

Remember, the aim here isn't to transform you into a Michelin-star chef overnight. The goal is to make cooking—and eating—a fun, satisfying, and ultimately rewarding experience that improves your relationship with food while keeping you nourished and energized.

You can create dishes that are both healthy and delicious, ensuring you maintain a balanced, high-protein, low-carb lifestyle without sacrificing flavor.

Ingredient Substitution Guide

To help you on your journey, here's a handy list of ingredient substitutions that maintain similar nutritional values. Use these swaps to adapt recipes to your needs without compromising on the healthy balance you're aiming for:

Proteins

- **Chicken / Turkey:** Both are lean, high in protein, and versatile in various dishes.
- **Lean Beef / Pork Tenderloin:** Opt for cuts that are lower in fat for a similar protein boost.
- **Tofu / Tempeh:** Excellent plant-based protein options that can often be used interchangeably.
- **Salmon / Tuna:** Both provide healthy omega-3 fats and are rich in protein.
- **Greek Yogurt / Cottage Cheese:** Great dairy sources of protein that can be swapped based on texture or flavor preference.

Carbohydrates

- **Quinoa / Farro:** Both whole grains are high in protein and fiber, offering a nutty flavor.
- **Sweet Potatoes / Butternut Squash:** Nutritious, complex carbs that provide steady energy.
- **Brown Rice / Wild Rice:** Both are hearty, fiber-rich options with a slightly different texture.
- **Oats / Barley:** A solid choice for breakfast or baking, offering similar fiber and nutrient profiles.

Fats

- **Avocado / Olive Oil (in dressings and dips):** Both offer heart-healthy fats; use avocado for a creamy texture and olive oil for a light drizzle.
- **Almonds / Walnuts:** Excellent sources of healthy fats and proteins that can be interchanged in snacks or recipes.
- **Chia Seeds / Flaxseeds:** Both are rich in omega-3 fatty acids and fiber; swap based on availability or desired texture.
- **Extra Virgin Olive Oil / Avocado Oil:** Both are great for cooking or dressing salads, offering a similar nutritional profile with slight flavor variations.

By using these substitutions, you can easily adapt recipes to what you have available, suit your taste preferences, or address specific dietary needs—all while keeping your meals balanced and in line with your high-protein, low-carb lifestyle.

Enjoy experimenting and making each recipe uniquely yours!

Getting Creative with Flavors

One of the joys of cooking is the opportunity to experiment with flavors and create dishes that truly excite your taste buds. Over time, I've learned that a healthy, high-protein, low-carb meal doesn't have to be bland or repetitive.
In fact, getting creative in the kitchen can transform even a simple recipe into a culinary adventure.

Embrace the Art of Flavor

1. **Experiment with Herbs and Spices:**
   Fresh herbs like basil, cilantro, and mint or spices like cumin, smoked paprika, and turmeric can completely change the character of a dish. I remember the first time I sprinkled a generous pinch of za'atar on my grilled chicken—it added a vibrant, earthy kick that turned an ordinary meal into something memorable.
2. **Mix Sweet and Savory Elements:**
   Combining a hint of natural sweetness with savory ingredients can lead to delightful surprises. For example, adding a drizzle of balsamic reduction or a few pomegranate seeds to a salad with lean protein not only enhances

the flavor but also creates a beautiful contrast of textures and tastes.

3. **Play with Acidity and Zest:**
   A splash of lemon or lime juice, or even a bit of zest, can brighten up a dish. When I'm preparing a high-protein fish dish, a squeeze of lemon not only enhances the flavor but also cuts through any richness, making the meal feel light and refreshing.

4. **Incorporate International Influences:**
   Don't be afraid to draw inspiration from cuisines around the world. Whether it's a Mediterranean twist with olives and feta, an Asian-inspired stir-fry with ginger and garlic, or a touch of Mexican flair with lime and chili, infusing your meals with diverse flavors can keep your taste buds on their toes and your meals interesting.

Practical Tips for Creative Cooking

1. **Start Small:**
   If you're new to flavor experimentation, begin by tweaking one or two elements in a familiar recipe. Add a new herb or try a different spice blend, and see how it transforms the dish.

2. **Taste as You Go:**
   One of the simplest yet most effective ways to build confidence in flavor creativity is to taste your food throughout the cooking process. This way, you can adjust seasonings gradually and avoid overwhelming your dish.

3. **Keep a Flavor Notebook:**
   I often jot down notes about what worked and what didn't in my recipes. Which spice combinations hit the mark? Which herbs added a burst of freshness? Keeping track of these discoveries helps me refine my approach and recreate successful dishes in the future.

4. **Don't Fear Mistakes:**
   Not every experiment will be a hit, and that's part of the fun. Each "mistake" is a learning opportunity that brings you closer to discovering your own signature flavors. Remember, cooking is as much about creativity as it is about nourishment.

A Personal Moment of Flavorful Discovery

I'll never forget the evening I decided to try something new with my usual grilled turkey. I was in the mood for something zesty and fresh, so I mixed a marinade of lemon juice, garlic, a sprinkle of rosemary, and a dash of chili flakes.

The result was a vibrant, tangy dish that not only elevated the turkey but also transformed a routine dinner into a delightful experience. That night, my family couldn't stop talking about how different and exciting the meal was. It was a clear reminder that a few creative tweaks could make all the difference in how we enjoy our food.

Final Thoughts

Getting creative with flavors is all about embracing experimentation and enjoying the process of discovery. The goal isn't to follow strict rules but to make your meals fun, satisfying, and uniquely yours.

As you grow more comfortable with different herbs, spices, and flavor combinations, you'll find that healthy cooking becomes a canvas for s elf-expression—one where every dish you create nourishes both your body and your soul. So go ahead, play with your ingredients, and let your taste buds guide you on this flavorful journey.

Enjoy the process, and remember: every new flavor is a step towards a more joyful, personalized approach to healthy eating.

A WEEK OF IDEAS: MY SAMPLE MENU

Imagine having a roadmap for the week—one that takes the guesswork out of what to eat while inspiring you with balanced, high-protein, low-carb meals. In this chapter, I'm excited to share my very own sample menu, a flexible plan that helped me transition from chaotic meal planning to a lifestyle where healthy eating feels effortless and enjoyable.

Over the years, I've learned that having a plan in place not only saves time but also builds confidence in the kitchen. This sample menu isn't meant to be a rigid schedule that you must follow exactly; rather, it's a source of inspiration and a starting point that you can adapt to fit your personal tastes, busy schedule, and even unexpected changes in your day.

In these pages, you'll find a day-by-day guide that balances lean proteins, nutrient-rich vegetables, and wholesome carbs in ways that keep your energy steady and your taste buds delighted.

Whether you're a working professional, a busy parent, or someone looking to simplify your cooking routine, this sample menu is designed to show you how easy it can be to prepare meals that are both nutritious and satisfying.

By using this menu as a blueprint, you'll discover new recipes, learn handy tips for meal prepping, and see firsthand how planning can transform your daily routine.

My goal is to help you feel empowered to take control of your eating habits—turning every meal into a moment of self-care, nourishment, and joy.

So, take a deep breath, relax, and get ready to explore a week full of ideas that will make healthy eating a delightful, stress-free part of your life.

Let's dive in and start planning meals that will leave you feeling energized, satisfied, and inspired every single day.

Structuring Seven Days of Varied Meals

Creating a week-long menu might seem daunting at first, but once you break it down, it becomes an exciting way to explore new recipes and keep your eating routine fresh. I've spent countless hours fine-tuning my weekly plan so that every day offers a balanced mix of high-protein, low-carb meals that are both delicious and energizing.

Here's a detailed look at how you can structure a seven-day menu that not only meets your nutritional needs but also keeps you inspired and satisfied throughout the week.

1. START WITH A FLEXIBLE FRAMEWORK

Daily Meal Breakdown:
Begin by deciding on a consistent structure for each day. Most days, I plan for three main meals—breakfast, lunch, and dinner—plus one or two snacks. This structure keeps my energy levels steady and prevents those mid-afternoon crashes.

Balanced Plate Concept:
Use the visual cue of a balanced plate for each meal: half should be filled with non-starchy vegetables, a quarter with lean protein, and the remaining quarter with healthy carbs or fats. This guideline helps ensure that every meal is well-rounded.

2. MIX UP THE THEMES

Variety is key to preventing boredom and ensuring you get a range of nutrients. Here's how I like to mix things up:

Protein Variety:
Alternate between different protein sources throughout the week. For example, plan for chicken on one day, fish on another, tofu or tempeh for a plant-based option, and perhaps lean beef or turkey on another day. This variety not only keeps your meals interesting but also exposes you to different amino acid profiles and flavors.

Carb and Vegetable Rotation:
Switch up your carb sources and vegetables. One day you might have quinoa paired with steamed broccoli, while another day you might opt for farro with a medley of bell peppers and zucchini. This helps ensure a wide range of vitamins, minerals, and fibers enter your diet.

International Flavors:
Infuse your menu with a few themed nights. Consider a Mediterranean-inspired meal one evening with grilled chicken, olive oil, and fresh salad, and an Asian-style stir-fry with ginger, garlic, and a splash of soy sauce another day. These small themes can make each day feel like a new culinary adventure.

3. PLAN FOR BREAKFAST, LUNCH, DINNER, AND SNACKS

Breakfast:
Aim for quick, high-protein breakfasts that set a positive tone for the day. Think smoothies, egg-based dishes, or Greek yogurt with berries. Rotate options to keep mornings exciting.

Lunch:
Plan lunches that are easy to pack and can be enjoyed both at home and on the go. Salads with lean protein, hearty wraps with low-carb tortillas, or bowls with pre-cooked grains and veggies are all great choices. If you're working outside the home, consider meals that travel well.

Dinner:
Dinners are your chance to experiment a little more. Think of recipes that allow you to unwind after a long day—grilled fish with roasted vegetables, a stir-fry that's full of color and crunch, or even a one-pan roasted chicken with a side of steamed greens. Make sure each dinner is designed to be both satisfying and easy to assemble, even on the busiest days.

Snacks:
Keep a couple of healthy snack options on hand. Nuts, cheese slices, vegetable sticks with hummus, or a small serving of cottage cheese can be lifesavers when hunger strikes between meals. Plan these in advance so you're not tempted by less nutritious options.

4. INCORPORATE MEAL PREPPING DAYS

Batch Cooking:
Dedicate a couple of hours during the weekend or on a quieter day to batch cook key ingredients. Grill a few chicken breasts, roast a variety of vegetables, or cook a large portion of quinoa. This way, you can mix and match components during the week to create different meals quickly.

Storage and Organization:
Invest in good quality, compartmentalized containers that keep prepped ingredients fresh. Label them by day or meal type, so when you're short on time, you know exactly what to grab.

5. STAY FLEXIBLE AND ADAPT

Plan with Room for Change:
Life is unpredictable—your schedule might change, or you might discover a new recipe you're excited to try. Build some flexibility into your plan by not over-scheduling every single meal. Allow for one or two "free" meals where you can experiment or simply enjoy a spontaneous choice.

Reflect and Adjust:
At the end of each week, take a moment to review what worked well and what could be improved. Did you have too many leftovers? Were some meals too time-consuming? Use these insights to tweak your plan for the next week, gradually honing in on what fits best with your lifestyle and tastes.

A Sample Week for Inspiration

Below is an example of a well-rounded, seven-day menu that not only keeps your meals varied but also makes use of versatile ingredients you can prepare in bulk.

This plan is designed to inspire you, offering balanced, high-protein, low-carb options that you can easily adapt based on what's available in your pantry and your personal preferences.

	MONDAY
BREAKFAST	Scrambled eggs with spinach and a side of Greek yogurt mixed with fresh berries and a sprinkle of chia seeds.
MORNING SNACK	Sliced cucumbers with a dollop of hummus.
LUNCH	Grilled chicken salad with mixed greens, cherry tomatoes, avocado, and a light vinaigrette.
AFTERNOON SNACK	A handful of almonds.
DINNER	Baked salmon served with quinoa and steamed broccoli, drizzled with lemon-tahini dressing.
OPTIONAL DESSERT	Fresh raspberries with a small dollop of whipped coconut cream.

	TUESDAY
BREAKFAST	A protein smoothie blended with almond milk, a scoop of protein powder, a small banana, and a tablespoon of peanut butter.

MORNING SNACK	Apple slices with a spoonful of almond butter.
LUNCH	Turkey lettuce wraps using pre-grilled turkey slices, avocado, shredded carrots, and a squeeze of lime.
AFTERNOON SNACK	Celery sticks paired with a low-carb cream cheese dip.
DINNER	Stir-fried tofu with mixed vegetables (broccoli, bell peppers, snap peas) served over a modest portion of brown rice.
OPTIONAL DESSERT	A small square of dark chocolate.

WEDNESDAY	
BREAKFAST	Greek yogurt parfait layered with mixed berries, a sprinkle of chia seeds, and a drizzle of honey.
MORNING SNACK	A hard-boiled egg and a few cherry tomatoes.
LUNCH	A quinoa bowl featuring grilled chicken, steamed kale, and roasted bell peppers, all tossed with a light lemon dressing.
AFTERNOON SNACK	A small handful of walnuts.
DINNER	Zucchini noodles topped with lean ground turkey and a rich marinara sauce, garnished with fresh basil.

OPTIONAL DESSERT	A serving of sugar-free gelatin topped with a light dollop of whipped cream.

THURSDAY	
BREAKFAST	Veggie omelet with mushrooms, spinach, and a sprinkle of feta cheese.
MORNING SNACK	Sliced bell peppers served with a side of guacamole.
LUNCH	Mixed greens salad topped with grilled salmon, avocado slices, and a squeeze of lemon.
AFTERNOON SNACK	A small cup of cottage cheese with sliced cucumber.
DINNER	Beef stir-fry with a medley of roasted vegetables (broccoli, carrots, snap peas) served over a small portion of wild rice.
OPTIONAL DESSERT	A fresh peach or another low-carb seasonal fruit.

FRIDAY	
BREAKFAST	Protein pancakes made with almond flour, served with a few fresh blueberries and a spoonful of Greek yogurt.
MORNING SNACK	A handful of mixed nuts (almonds, walnuts, pecans).

LUNCH	Chicken and avocado wrap using a low-carb tortilla, filled with grilled chicken, lettuce, tomato, and a light mustard dressing.
AFTERNOON SNACK	Sliced apple paired with a small serving of cheese.
DINNER	Baked cod with a side of roasted Brussels sprouts and a quinoa salad tossed in a light vinaigrette.
OPTIONAL DESSERT	A serving of low-carb ice cream or another sugar-free treat.

SATURDAY	
BREAKFAST	A spinach and egg white frittata loaded with chopped vegetables and a sprinkle of Parmesan cheese.
MORNING SNACK	A low-carb protein bar.
LUNCH	A vibrant salad featuring mixed greens, sliced turkey, cherry tomatoes, and cucumbers, dressed with olive oil and vinegar.
AFTERNOON SNACK	Sliced radishes with a dollop of guacamole.
DINNER	Shrimp and vegetable skewers (using bell peppers, zucchini, and red onions) served over a bed of cauliflower rice.
OPTIONAL DESSERT	Fresh strawberries drizzled with a touch of dark chocolate.

SUNDAY	
BREAKFAST	Chia pudding made with unsweetened almond milk, topped with a mix of berries and a sprinkle of sliced almonds.
MORNING SNACK	A hard-boiled egg paired with a few slices of avocado.
LUNCH	A hearty bowl of vegetable soup enriched with lean beef and plenty of l ow-carb veggies, accompanied by a side salad.
AFTERNOON SNACK	A small handful of pistachios.
DINNER	A Mediterranean-style grilled chicken dish served with roasted eggplant and a small portion of farro, garnished with fresh herbs.
OPTIONAL DESSERT	A light, sugar-free yogurt parfait with a sprinkle of cinnamon.

Final Thoughts on Your Sample Week

Remember, this sample week is just one example of a typical eating plan from my own journey—it's not a strict guideline for what you must eat. Later in this book, you'll discover a wealth of recipes, along with a complete 30-day meal plan and a comprehensive list of approved foods for this high-protein, low-carb lifestyle. This way, you can mix and match meals according to your personal tastes, schedule, and nutritional needs.

I've provided this sample week to show you that it's possible to enjoy a variety of delicious, satisfying meals while spending very little time on preparation. Use it as inspiration to see how flexible and enjoyable healthy eating can be.

Enjoy the journey and happy cooking!

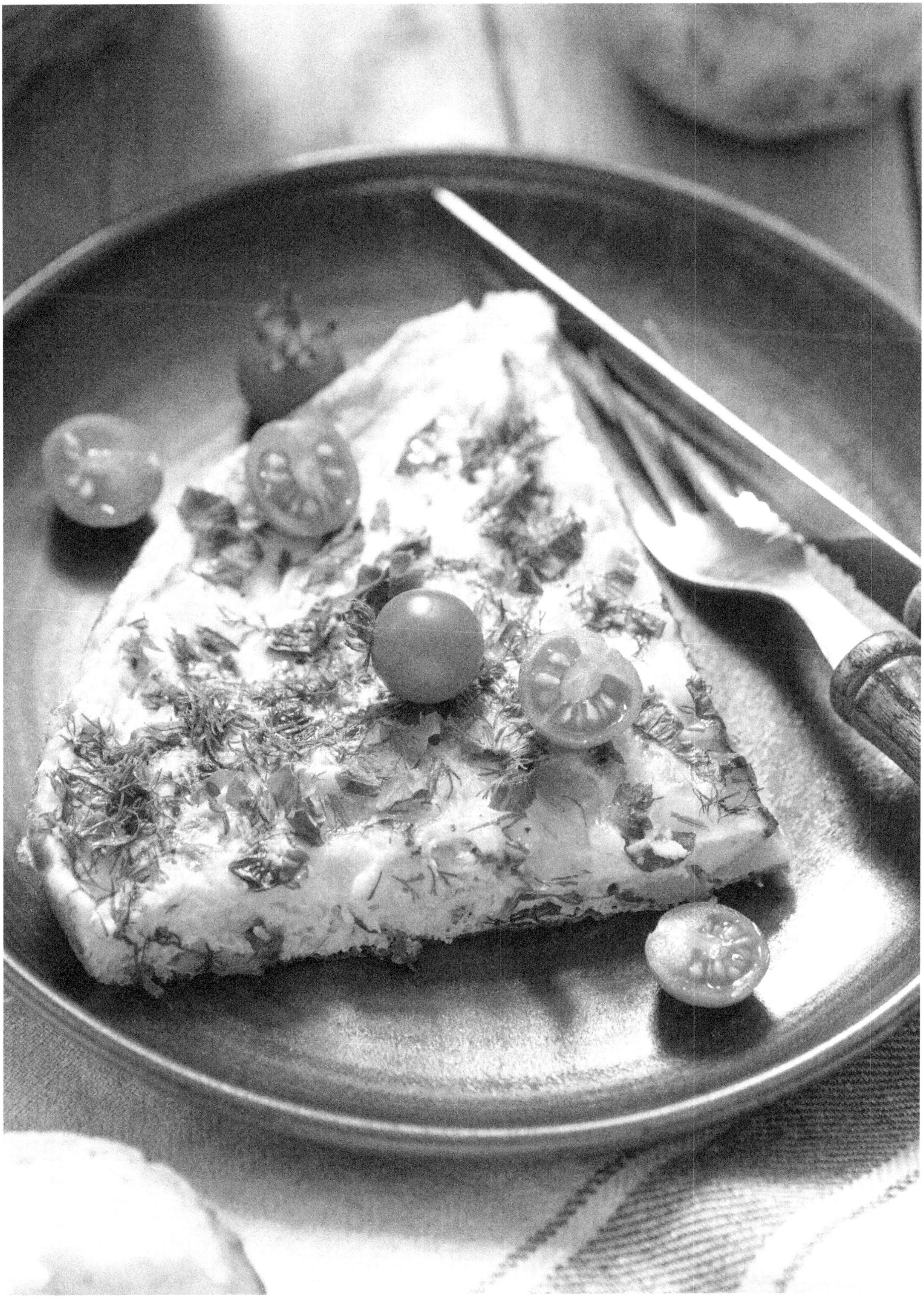

Tailoring the Plan to Your Daily Routine

Every day is different, and your meal plan should work with your life, not against it. I've learned that a successful, sustainable eating plan is one that flexes with your schedule and adapts to your personal habits. Whether you're juggling a busy work schedule, managing family commitments, or carving out time for self-care, tailoring your meal plan to your daily routine is the key to making healthy eating effortless.

Understanding Your Unique Schedule

Start by taking a close look at your day-to-day routine. When do you usually wake up? When do you have time for a sit-down meal? Are there parts of your day when you're more likely to be on the go? By mapping out your day, you can identify the optimal times for meals and snacks. For example, if you're someone who finds mornings rushed, consider preparing a grab-and-go breakfast the night before, such as a protein-packed smoothie or overnight oats.

Flexibility is Essential

Your plan doesn't have to be rigid. Some days, you might have more time to experiment with a new recipe; other days, you might need something ultra-quick. Build flexibility into your weekly plan by having a few "fast-track" options that you can rely on during busy times. Perhaps on hectic days, you can rely on pre-cooked proteins and roasted vegetables that you've prepared in advance. On days when you have a little extra time, try out a new, more elaborate dish.

Practical Tips for Customizing Your Plan

1. **Plan Ahead:** Spend a few minutes at the start of each week reviewing your calendar. Identify any days where your routine might be disrupted, and plan simpler meals or extra snacks for those times.
2. **Batch Cooking:** Prepare versatile ingredients—like grilled chicken, quinoa, or chopped vegetables—in larger quantities. These can be quickly assembled into different meals, ensuring you always have a nutritious option ready, no matter how hectic the day gets.
3. **Keep It Simple:** Don't overcomplicate your meals if you know you'll be short on time. A salad with a good protein source and a handful of nuts can be just as satisfying as a multi-course dish.
4. **Listen to Your Body:** If you're hungry earlier than expected or need a quick energy boost, adjust your plan. It's important that your meal schedule supports your natural rhythms and keeps you energized throughout the day.

A Personal Insight

I used to follow a strict meal schedule that left little room for spontaneity—until I realized that life rarely goes as planned. One busy week, I found myself with back-to-back meetings and unexpected errands. Instead of stressing over a missed meal, I leaned on my batch-cooked proteins and pre-cut vegetables to throw together a quick stir-fry that saved the day.

That experience taught me that flexibility isn't just a convenience—it's a necessity. Adapting your plan to fit your unique daily routine not only makes healthy eating more manageable but also more enjoyable.

The Takeaway

Tailoring your meal plan to your daily routine is about creating a structure that works for you. It means designing a flexible framework where healthy eating becomes second nature, no matter what your day holds. As you move forward, experiment with different strategies and adjust your plan as needed.

Remember, the ultimate goal is to make your meals a source of nourishment and joy that seamlessly integrates into your lifestyle. Enjoy the process of making your plan truly your own!

RECIPES: THE BASICS BEFORE YOU HEAD TO THE STOVE

Before you dive into the exciting world of high-protein, low-carb recipes, it's essential to build a strong foundation that makes your time in the kitchen both enjoyable and efficient. In this chapter, we're going to cover the basics that will set you up for success every time you cook. Think of it as your culinary toolkit—a set of simple strategies and practical tips that will help you streamline your cooking process, boost your confidence, and ensure that every meal you prepare is as delicious as it is nourishing.

What This Chapter Offers

- **Foundational Techniques:** We'll start by discussing some key cooking techniques that are essential for creating healthy, flavorful dishes. Whether it's how to properly sauté vegetables to retain their crunch and nutrients, or mastering the art of quick protein preparation, these techniques are designed to make your cooking experience smoother.
- **Setting Up Your Workspace:** A well-organized kitchen can make a world of difference. We'll explore how to set up your workstation for maximum efficiency—from arranging your tools and ingredients (mise en place) to choosing the right kitchen gadgets that save you time without sacrificing quality.
- **Understanding Recipe Structure:** Recipes are more than just a list of ingredients—they're a roadmap to creating a meal that fits your nutritional goals. I'll walk you through how to read and interpret recipes, break them down into manageable steps, and even customize them to match your personal taste and busy schedule.
- **Time-Saving Tips and Tricks:** One of my favorite parts of cooking is discovering small hacks that make the process faster and more enjoyable. In this chapter, you'll find practical advice on how to prep in advance, use efficient cooking methods, and make the most of your ingredients—so you can spend less time in the kitchen and more time enjoying your meals.
- **The Joy of Cooking:** Most importantly, this chapter is about making cooking a fun, rewarding experience. Healthy eating shouldn't feel like a chore or a set of rigid rules—it should be a creative, uplifting activity that brings a sense of accomplishment and joy. I want you to see this as an opportunity to experiment, express yourself, and develop a healthier relationship with food.

Why These Basics Matter

Learning the fundamentals before you jump into recipes not only builds your confidence but also helps ensure that your meals turn out just the way you want them. When you're equipped with the right techniques and a well-organized kitchen, even the most complex recipes become approachable and manageable. This chapter is designed to take the guesswork out of cooking so that you can focus on what really matters: creating meals that are both delicious and aligned with your high-protein, low-carb lifestyle.

So, take a moment, breathe, and get ready to transform your cooking routine. With these essentials under your belt, you'll soon find that heading to the stove is not only less intimidating but also a source of creativity, nourishment, and pleasure.

Let's get started on building a solid culinary foundation that will support you every time you step into the kitchen!

Making the Most of Your 30 Minutes in the Kitchen

Imagine this: You come home after a long, busy day, and you still want a nutritious, high-protein, low-carb meal without spending hours in the kitchen. Believe it or not, 30 minutes is all you need—and I'm here to show you how.

When I first set out to simplify my cooking routine, I was skeptical. I thought, "How can I possibly prepare a satisfying, healthy meal in just half an hour?"

But with a bit of planning and a few handy techniques, I discovered that 30 minutes can be plenty of time to create dishes that are both delicious and nourishing. Let me walk you through some strategies and real-life examples that might just change the way you think about cooking.

Plan Ahead for Speed and Success

- **Prep in Advance:** Spend a little time during the weekend or on a quieter day to wash, chop, or marinate key ingredients. For instance, I often grill a batch of chicken breasts and roast a tray of mixed vegetables. Then, on busy evenings, I simply reheat these components and quickly assemble a meal—turning a 30-minute dinner into a reality.
- **Keep a Well-Stocked Pantry:** Having essentials like canned beans, whole grains (like quinoa), and

your favorite spices on hand means you can whip up a meal without making a special trip to the store. When you're prepared, you're less stressed and more efficient.

Efficient Cooking Techniques

- **One-Pan Meals:** One of my go-to methods is a one-pan dinner. I might toss pre-cut veggies, a protein like fish or tofu, and a drizzle of olive oil onto a sheet pan, season everything well, and roast it in the oven. While the pan does the work for you, you can focus on setting the table or simply unwinding.
- **Stir-Frying:** Stir-fries are incredibly quick. Heat up a wok or a large non-stick skillet, add a splash of oil, throw in your protein and colorful veggies, and stir-fry until just tender. A splash of soy sauce or a squeeze of lime can elevate the dish in minutes. This method not only saves time but also locks in nutrients and flavors.
- **Quick Boil and Steam:** For meals like quinoa bowls or steamed fish, bringing water to a boil quickly and using a steamer basket can reduce cooking time dramatically. In 20-30 minutes, you can have perfectly cooked grains and tender, flavorful proteins.

Real-Life Example

I remember one hectic Tuesday when I barely had time to breathe between work calls and family duties. Instead of resorting to takeout, I decided to make a quick shrimp stir-fry. I grabbed a pre-cooked bag of frozen shrimp, a mix of fresh veggies I'd prepped earlier in the week, and a bottle of low-sodium stir-fry sauce. Within 30 minutes, I had a vibrant, satisfying meal on the table.

That evening, not only did I enjoy a delicious dinner, but I also felt proud for taking charge of my health without compromising on flavor.

Tips to Maximize Your 30 Minutes

- **Set a Timer:** Challenge yourself by setting a timer for each phase—prep, cooking, and plating. This keeps you focused and helps build your speed over time.
- **Stay Organized:** Before you start, make sure everything you need is within arm's reach. This "mise en place" not only speeds up the process but also makes it enjoyable.

- **Keep It Simple:** You don't need elaborate techniques to create a memorable meal. Sometimes, a few simple ingredients, cooked well, can be more satisfying than a complicated dish that takes hours.

The Bigger Picture

Remember, the goal isn't to transform you into a gourmet chef in 30 minutes—it's to show you that with a little planning and the right techniques, you can enjoy healthy, high-protein, low-carb meals without feeling rushed. These 30 minutes are your time to nourish your body, boost your energy, and maybe even find a little joy in the process of cooking.

So, embrace the challenge and see these 30 minutes as a gift—an opportunity to reclaim control over your meals and your health. With each quick, delicious dish you create, you'll build confidence and discover that healthy eating can be both effortless and incredibly satisfying.

Enjoy every moment at your stove, knowing that you're making a positive choice for your well-being.

Keeping an Eye on Protein and Carb Counts

Let's face it—tracking every single gram of protein and carbs can feel tedious, but there are practical ways to keep your intake in check without turning your kitchen routine into a science experiment. Here are some real-world strategies I've found incredibly useful, allowing me to stay on track while keeping things simple and stress-free.

Use Visual Portion Guides

- **Protein Portions:** Instead of weighing every piece of chicken or tofu, I rely on a simple trick: a palm-sized portion roughly equals a serving of lean protein. Over time, I've learned that keeping this visual reference in mind helps me naturally build balanced meals without constant measuring.
- **Carb Portions:** For complex carbs like quinoa or sweet potatoes, I use my fist as a guide. This visual cue works well when you're preparing your plate quickly and don't have time to measure exactly.

Pre-Portion When Meal Prepping

- **Batch Cooking Benefits:** When you're preparing your meals in advance, portion out your proteins and carbs into individual containers. Label them if needed. For example, when I grill chicken breasts on Sunday, I divide them into portions that I know are just right for one meal. This not only saves time during the week but also gives you a clear idea of how much you're eating.
- **Standardized Recipes:** Choose recipes that come with suggested portion sizes and stick to them until you're comfortable with your own adjustments. Over time, you'll internalize these standards, making it easier to eyeball the right amounts without detailed tracking.

Smart Use of Technology

- **Simple Tracking Tools:** If you want a bit more precision without overwhelming yourself, consider using a user-friendly app or even a quick note on your phone. Instead of logging every ingredient, simply note down when you've met your daily protein and carb targets. This approach helps you stay aware without turning meal planning into a full-time job.
- **Digital Reminders:** Set a weekly reminder to review your meal portions. Reflecting on what you ate can help you fine-tune your instincts about portion sizes, making the process more intuitive over time.

Practical Kitchen Habits

- **Familiarize Yourself with Common Foods:** Over time, you'll start to remember that a standard chicken breast or a cup of cooked quinoa provides a reliable amount of protein or carbs. When you're comfortable with these benchmarks, checking your intake becomes second nature.
- **Keep a Mini Cheat Sheet:** Write down a few quick reference points—like "one medium egg ≈ 6g protein" or "1/2 cup quinoa ≈ 4g protein"—and stick it on your fridge. This little guide can be a lifesaver when you're in a rush and need a quick refresher.

A Note on Calorie Counting for Weight Loss

If weight loss is one of your goals, you might find that keeping an eye on your calorie intake becomes even more essential. In this case, it's a good idea to consult with a specialist who can help determine the exact amounts of food you should be consuming to reach your specific weight loss objectives. The great news is that all of the recipes in this book come with detailed nutritional information per serving.

That means you'll have ready access to the amounts of protein, carbohydrates, fats, and total calories in each dish—helping you stay mindful of your intake without the guesswork.

The Bottom Line

The goal isn't to transform you into a calorie-counting expert; it's to help you develop a mindful approach to eating that supports your high-protein, low-carb lifestyle. By using visual cues, pre-portioned meals, and a few tech tools, you can keep an eye on your macros without getting bogged down in numbers.

This practical, no-fuss method lets you enjoy your food and maintain your energy throughout the day—leaving you more time to focus on what truly matters. Remember, these strategies are here to make your life easier. Over time, you'll find that a little awareness goes a long way in building balanced meals, and soon tracking your macros will become a natural part of your routine.

Enjoy the process, keep it simple, and adjust as needed—your health and happiness depend on it!

FOOD VARIATIONS AND EATING ON THE GO

Life doesn't always allow for long, leisurely meals—sometimes you're on the move, rushing from work to school to errands, and you need to eat well without slowing down. This chapter is all about how to adapt your high-protein, low-carb eating plan for a busy lifestyle. I'm excited to share practical strategies and personal insights that have helped me stay on track even on the most hectic days.

Adapting to Life's Curveballs

Not every day will be spent in a fully-equipped kitchen. There are days when you might need a quick bite between meetings or a portable meal during a

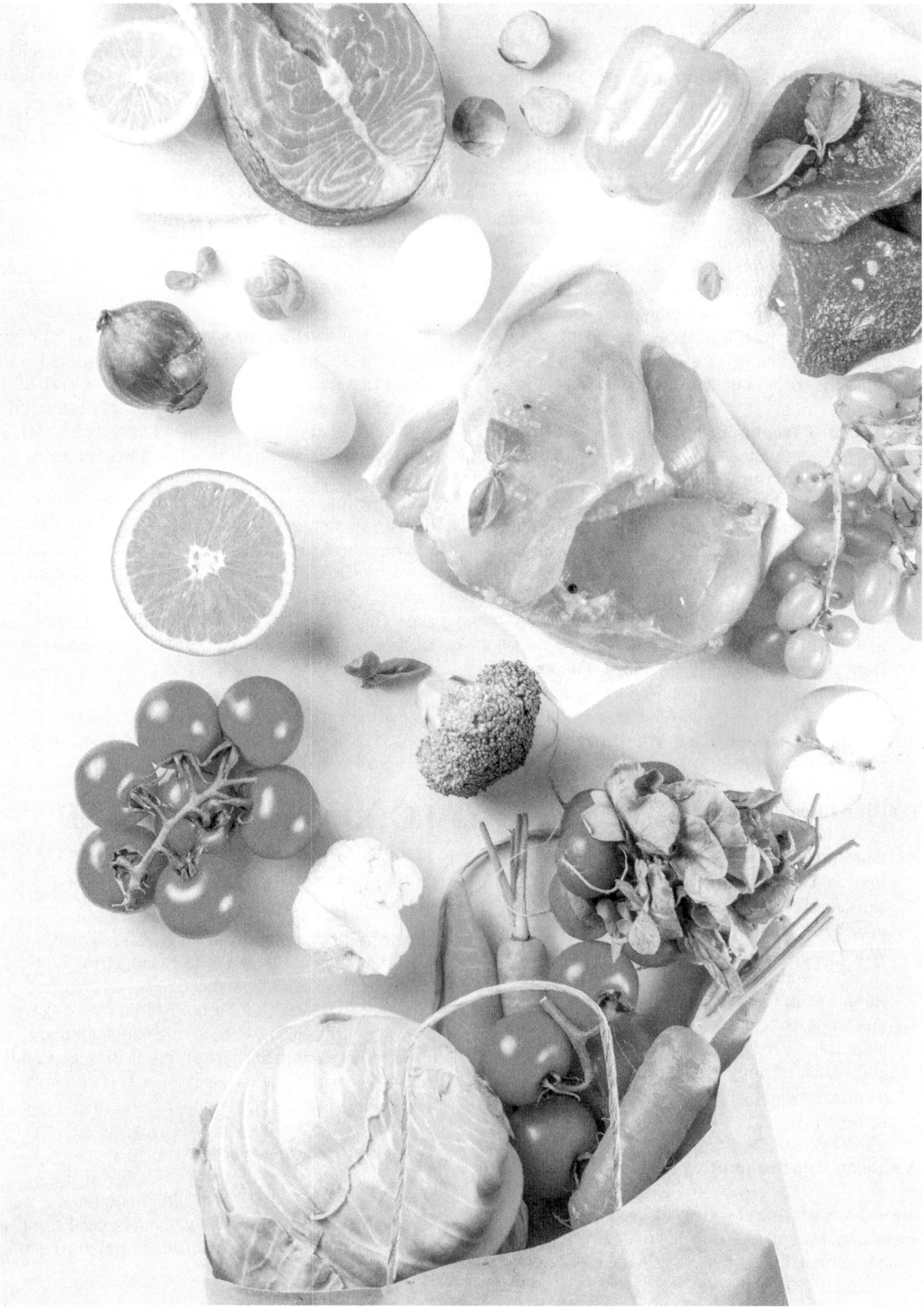

road trip. I've learned that with a little planning and creativity, you can enjoy healthy, satisfying meals wherever you are.

For instance, I once found myself in the middle of a long day of conferences with no time for a sit-down lunch. Instead of defaulting to fast food, I packed a container of grilled chicken, mixed greens, and a small serving of quinoa—all prepped the night before. That simple habit kept me energized and focused without the heavy feeling of a fast-food meal.

Strategies for Eating on the Go

- **Plan and Pre-Prep:** A little preparation goes a long way. Consider spending a few hours on the weekend prepping versatile ingredients like grilled proteins, roasted vegetables, and cooked grains. These can be quickly assembled into a variety of meals during the week—whether it's a hearty salad, a wrap, or a simple bowl.
- **Portable Containers and Snacks:** Invest in quality, leak-proof containers and portable snack options. Pre-portioning nuts, cheese, or veggie sticks into small bags makes it easier to grab a healthy snack when you're in a rush. I always keep a few of these on hand in my bag or car.
- **Creative Meal Variations:** One of the best parts of this lifestyle is learning how to vary your meals using similar ingredients. For example, the grilled chicken you prepare in bulk can be sliced for a wrap one day, added to a salad the next, or even turned into a quick stir-fry with fresh veggies later on. This flexibility not only keeps your meals interesting but also saves time and reduces food waste.
- **Restaurant Strategies:** When dining out, don't be afraid to ask for modifications. Many restaurants are willing to substitute a side of steamed vegetables for fries or to grill your protein instead of frying it. Reviewing the menu ahead of time and choosing options that align with your high-protein, low-carb approach can make dining out less stressful and more enjoyable.

Practical Tips for Variation

- **Switch It Up:** Keep a list of interchangeable ingredients that provide similar nutritional benefits. For instance, if you're out of quinoa, try farro; if grilled chicken isn't available, turkey might be a good alternative. This way, you're never stuck when life gets busy.
- **Use Sauces and Dressings Wisely:** A flavorful dressing or sauce can completely transform a simple meal. When you're on the go, having a few healthy, portable dressings in a small container can help elevate a basic salad or wrap.
- **Mix and Match:** Experiment with different combinations of proteins, vegetables, and healthy fats. You might have a go-to mix for a salad, but try varying the toppings or the seasoning throughout the week to keep your palate excited.

A Personal Note

I've had plenty of days when work or family commitments meant I couldn't spend much time in the kitchen. I learned that even on the busiest days, a little planning makes it possible to enjoy a healthy, delicious meal without feeling rushed or compromised. Whether it's a well-prepared snack or a complete meal, these strategies have not only helped me maintain my energy and focus but also deepened my enjoyment of food—even on the go.

Final Thoughts

Remember, eating well while on the move is entirely achievable. With a bit of foresight, creative meal planning, and a willingness to adapt, you can stick to your high-protein, low-carb lifestyle no matter where you are. Embrace these strategies as part of your everyday routine, and soon you'll find that healthy eating becomes a natural, satisfying part of your busy life—leaving you energized and ready to tackle whatever comes your way.

Enjoy the journey and keep exploring new ways to make healthy choices, even when time is short!

Simple Ingredient Swaps

One of the easiest ways to keep your meals interesting and adaptable—especially when you're on the go—is to master the art of simple ingredient swaps. Over time, I've discovered that swapping out one ingredient for another can be a game-changer.

It not only keeps your dishes varied and exciting but also helps you stay on track with your high-protein, low-carb goals without feeling limited by what's available in your pantry.

Why Ingredient Swaps Work

Ingredient swaps are all about flexibility. Life can be unpredictable, and sometimes your go-to ingredients might not be available, or you might simply crave a new flavor twist. By knowing which ingredients offer similar nutritional benefits and textures, you can easily adapt recipes to suit your taste and schedule. This strategy turns potential obstacles into opportunities to experiment and personalize your meals.

Practical Examples of Swaps

- **Proteins:** If a recipe calls for chicken but you're in the mood for something different—or if chicken isn't available—you can swap it for turkey. Both are lean proteins that work beautifully in salads, wraps, or stir-fries. I also love exchanging tofu for tempeh when I want a plant-based option with a bit more texture.
- **Carbohydrates:** For a hearty grain base, quinoa is a favorite of mine. But if you find yourself without it, farro makes a fantastic alternative. Both provide a similar protein boost and fiber content, with a slightly nutty flavor that pairs well with a variety of dishes. Similarly, if a recipe uses sweet potatoes, you can often substitute butternut squash for a similar level of natural sweetness and nutritional benefits.
- **Vegetables and Sides:** When it comes to veggies, flexibility is key. For instance, if a dish calls for broccoli but you'd prefer a different texture or flavor, try swapping in cauliflower. They're both low in carbs and provide a great crunch when roasted or steamed.
- **Fats:** Healthy fats are essential in our meals, and you can easily swap sources. If you're using avocado oil in a dressing and find it isn't available, extra virgin olive oil is a reliable alternative that offers a similar nutritional profile and robust flavor.

A Personal Swap Story

I remember one busy afternoon when I was preparing a quick lunch. I had planned to make a quinoa salad with grilled chicken and roasted vegetables. However, when I got to the store, I realized they were out of quinoa. Instead of feeling frustrated, I recalled that I had some farro in my pantry from a previous batch meal prep.
I decided to swap quinoa for farro, and the result was surprisingly delightful. The farro added a slightly chewier texture that perfectly complemented the tender chicken and crisp vegetables. That day, I learned that being flexible and creative with ingredient swaps not only saved me time but also opened up a whole new range of flavors in my meals.

Tips for Successful Ingredient Swaps

- **Know Your Nutritional Goals:** Make sure the ingredient you're swapping in maintains the high-protein, low-carb profile you're aiming for. Familiarize yourself with the nutritional content of common ingredients to make informed decisions.
- **Experiment Gradually:** Start with small swaps in recipes you're already comfortable with. As you gain confidence, you can experiment with more significant changes and even develop your own signature versions of classic dishes.
- **Keep a List:** I keep a small list of my favorite ingredient swaps handy—so if I'm missing something, I know exactly what to reach for. This list evolves over time as I discover new combinations that work well together.
- **Taste and Adjust:** Every time you swap an ingredient, taste your dish as you go. Small adjustments in seasoning might be necessary to balance the new flavors, but that's part of the fun of culinary creativity.

Allowed Foods and Foods to Avoid in a High-Protein, Low-Carb Lifestyle

Here's a quick reference list of foods that work well with a high-protein, low-carb regime and those you might want to steer clear of. This guide is divided into three key categories: Proteins, Carbohydrates, and Fats.

PROTEINS

Allowed:
- Lean Meats: Chicken breast, turkey, lean cuts of beef and pork tenderloin.
- Seafood: Salmon, tuna, cod, shrimp, and other white fish.
- Eggs: Whole eggs and egg whites
- Dairy: Greek yogurt, cottage cheese, and low-fat milk.
- Plant-Based Options: Tofu, tempeh, and edamame; legumes in moderation if they fit within your carb limits.

Foods to Avoid:
- Processed Meats: Sausages, hot dogs, bacon, and deli meats loaded with preservatives and high sodium
- High-Fat, Low-Quality Proteins: Fatty cuts of red meat that contribute excessive saturated fat

CARBOHYDRATES

Allowed:
- Non-Starchy Vegetables: Leafy greens, broccoli, cauliflower, zucchini, bell peppers, asparagus, etc.
- Low-Sugar Fruits: Berries, green apples, citrus fruits (in moderation).
- Whole Grains (in Limited Portions): Quinoa, farro, barley, and oats.
- Legumes (in Moderation): Lentils, chickpeas, and other beans—if they fit within your overall carb goals.

Foods to Avoid:
- Refined Carbs: White bread, white rice, pasta made from refined flour.
- Sugary Foods: Pastries, desserts, sugary cereals, and other processed foods high in added sugars.

FATS

Allowed:
- Healthy Oils: Extra virgin olive oil, avocado oil.
- Whole Foods: Avocados, nuts, seeds, and nut butters (without added sugars).
- Fatty Fish: Salmon, mackerel, and other fish rich in omega-3 fatty acids.

Foods to Avoid:
- Trans Fats: Hydrogenated oils and highly processed snacks.
- Excessive Saturated Fats: Deep-fried foods, high-fat processed meats, and margarine.

The Big Picture

Simple ingredient swaps are a powerful tool in your cooking arsenal. They empower you to adapt to whatever life throws your way—whether it's a missing ingredient, a craving for a different flavor, or simply the need for variety in your routine. With these swaps, you can keep your high-protein, low-carb meals exciting, nutritious, and perfectly suited to your busy lifestyle.

Embrace these opportunities to get creative, and remember that every swap is a chance to make your meals uniquely yours. Enjoy the freedom to experiment, and let your taste buds lead you to delicious new discoveries!

Handling Social Events and Restaurant Dining

Navigating social events and dining out can be a challenge when you're committed to a high-protein, low-carb lifestyle—but it's far from impossible. With a little planning and a flexible mindset, you can enjoy gatherings, celebrations, or even a casual dinner out without compromising your nutritional goals. In fact, managing your choices in these situations can not only help you stay on track but also serve as inspiration for others.

EMBRACE THE SOCIAL EXPERIENCE

Enjoy the Moment:
Social events are about connection and fun. Remember, one meal or one evening won't derail your progress. Enjoy yourself and indulge a little if you need to—balance is key, and occasional deviations are part of a healthy lifestyle.

Plan Ahead Mentally:
Before you head out, take a moment to decide how you want to approach the meal. Set realistic expectations, knowing that making the best choices available in the moment is enough. This mindset reduces stress and helps you fully engage in the social experience.

SMART STRATEGIES FOR DINING OUT

Review the Menu:
When possible, look up the restaurant's menu in a dvance. Identify dishes that emphasize lean proteins, vegetables, and healthier sides. Don't hesitate to ask for modifications, like swapping fries for a side salad or opting for grilled instead of fried options.

Portion Control:
Restaurant portions can be generous. Consider sharing an entrée or asking for a to-go box at the start of your meal so you can portion out what you'll eat. This helps you maintain control without feeling deprived.

NAVIGATING ALCOHOL AND SOCIAL DRINKING

Alcohol can be a part of social occasions without sabotaging your high-protein, low-carb lifestyle—if approached mindfully.

Choose Wisely:
Opt for lighter options like a glass of wine, a light beer, or a spirit mixed with soda water and a splash of lemon. These choices generally have fewer carbs and calories compared to sugary cocktails or heavy beers.

Moderation is Key:
Enjoying a drink or two is perfectly acceptable. Alcohol in moderation doesn't make you negative—it shows that you can balance social indulgence with a commitment to your health goals. In fact, being mindful about your drinking habits can inspire your friends and family to adopt a more balanced lifestyle, too.

Alternate and Hydrate:
Consider alternating alcoholic beverages with water or sparkling water. This not only helps keep you hydrated but also slows down your alcohol consumption, allowing you to enjoy the social setting without overindulging.

Healthy Substitutions:
If you're looking to avoid alcohol altogether, many restaurants now offer creative non-alcoholic cocktails or "mocktails" that are flavorful and satisfying. Choosing these alternatives can still let you join in the fun without compromising your nutritional goals.

A Personal Experience

I remember a time at a family reunion when I was initially nervous about dining out and drinking in a social setting. I decided to stick with my high-protein, low-carb choices by selecting a grilled fish entrée and a side salad. When it came to drinks, I opted for a glass of dry red wine—knowing it was a lighter choice—and alternated it with water. Not only did I feel great the next day, but several family members commented on how balanced and energetic I seemed.

That day, I realized that managing your choices in social settings isn't about restriction—it's about making mindful decisions that let you enjoy life without compromise. In fact, these healthy habits can set an example and inspire others to approach social eating and drinking with balance and awareness.

Final Thoughts

Handling social events and restaurant dining is about balance, flexibility, and enjoying the experience without guilt. Whether you're making smart menu choices, managing portion sizes, or navigating alcohol with mindfulness, every decision you make contributes to a larger, sustainable healthy lifestyle.

Embrace these strategies, knowing that one evening or one drink won't derail your progress. Instead, let your balanced approach be a source of inspiration for those around you, proving that you can enjoy life's social moments while staying true to your health goals.

Enjoy your meals, connect with others, and remember: your journey is about overall balance, not perfection.

ENERGIZING BREAKFASTS

Breakfast isn't just another meal—it's the spark that ignites your energy and sets the tone for the entire day. In a high-protein, low-carb lifestyle, a well-crafted breakfast can help stabilize your blood sugar, curb cravings, and keep you feeling full and focused well into the morning.

Whether you're rushing off to work or easing into a relaxed weekend, these energizing recipes are designed to be quick, delicious, and incredibly satisfying.

By starting your day with a meal that packs both flavor and nutrition, you're not only fueling your body but also nurturing your overall well-being. These recipes, created with simplicity in mind, use no more than six ingredients and can be prepared in 30 minutes or less—leaving you extra time to enjoy the day ahead.

Embrace the power of breakfast and discover how a few creative, high-protein, low-carb dishes can transform your morning routine into a moment of joy and vitality.

Sunrise Energy Omelette

Servings: 1 person

Prep Time: 15 minutes (including cooking)

Ingredients:
- 3 large eggs
- 1/2 cup fresh spinach (roughly chopped)
- 1/4 cup diced red bell pepper
- 1 tablespoon olive oil
- Salt, to taste
- Pepper, to taste

Possible Variations:
You can experiment by adding 1/4 cup of diced onion with the vegetables for extra flavor or by sprinkling a small amount of low-fat cheese on top before folding the omelette. Another great twist is to mix in a tablespoon of plain Greek yogurt with the eggs for a creamier texture.

Preparation:
1. Heat a non-stick skillet over medium heat and add 1 tablespoon of olive oil.
2. Add the chopped spinach and diced red bell pepper to the skillet, and sauté for about 3 minutes until slightly softened.
3. While the vegetables are cooking, whisk the 3 eggs in a bowl with a pinch of salt and pepper.
4. Pour the beaten eggs over the sautéed vegetables in the skillet and allow the edges to set for about 2–3 minutes.
5. Once the omelette is mostly set, gently fold it in half and cook for an additional 1–2 minutes until fully cooked.
6. Transfer the omelette to a plate and enjoy your energizing breakfast!

Nutritional Info (per serving): kcal 250 | pro 20g | carbs 5g | fat 16g

---

Berry Burst Bliss Parfait

Servings: 1 person

Prep Time: 5 minutes (including assembly)

Ingredients:
- 1 cup plain Greek yogurt
- 1/2 cup mixed fresh berries (blueberries, strawberries, raspberries)
- 1 tablespoon chopped almonds
- 1 teaspoon honey (optional)

Possible Variations:
You can swap chopped almonds with walnuts or pecans, or add a dash of cinnamon for an extra flavor twist.

Preparation:
1. In a serving glass, combine all the ingredients by layering 1 cup of Greek yogurt, 1/2 cup of mixed berries, and a drizzle of honey if desired.
2. Top with 1 tablespoon of chopped almonds and serve immediately.

Nutritional Info (per serving): kcal 220 | pro 20g | carbs 15g | fat 8g

Green Glow Egg Muffins

Servings: 4 muffins

Prep Time: 25 minutes (including baking)

Ingredients:
- 6 large eggs
- 1/2 cup chopped fresh spinach
- 1/4 cup diced green bell pepper
- 1/4 cup shredded low-fat cheddar cheese
- Salt, to taste
- Pepper, to taste

Possible Variations:
For a twist, replace the cheddar with feta or mix in some diced tomatoes with the spinach and bell pepper.

Preparation:
1. Preheat your oven to 350°F.
2. In a bowl, combine all the ingredients by whisking the eggs together with salt and pepper, then stirring in the spinach, green bell pepper, and cheddar cheese.
3. Pour the mixture evenly into a greased muffin tin (yielding 4 muffins) and bake for 18–20 minutes until the muffins are set and lightly golden.

Nutritional Info (per muffin): kcal 90 | pro 8g | carbs 1g | fat 6g

Almond Dream Pancakes

Servings: 1 serving (yields 3 small pancakes)

Prep Time: 20 minutes

Ingredients:
- 1/2 cup almond flour
- 1 large egg
- 1/4 cup unsweetened almond milk
- 1/4 cup chopped almonds
- A pinch of salt (optional)

Possible Variations:
Feel free to swap the chopped almonds with walnuts or pecans, or add a dash of cinnamon to enhance the flavor.

Preparation:
1. In a bowl, combine all the ingredients by mixing almond flour, egg, unsweetened almond milk, and a pinch of salt until you have a smooth batter; then gently fold in the chopped almonds.
2. Heat a non-stick skillet over medium heat, lightly coat with cooking spray, and cook small rounds of the batter for 2–3 minutes on each side until golden and set.
3. Remove from the skillet and serve warm.

Nutritional Info (per serving): kcal 300 | pro 15g | carbs 10g | fat 22g

Supercharged Morning Smoothie Bowl

Servings: 1 person

Prep Time: 10 minutes

Ingredients:
- 1 cup unsweetened almond milk
- 1 scoop vanilla protein powder
- 1/2 cup frozen mixed berries
- 1/4 cup frozen spinach
- 1/4 avocado

Possible Variations:
You may substitute frozen spinach with kale or add a topping of chopped nuts for extra crunch. Enjoy experimenting to make this smoothie bowl uniquely yours!

Preparation:
1. Place all the ingredients into a blender and blend on high until the mixture is smooth and creamy.
2. Pour the smoothie into a bowl and serve immediately.

Nutritional Info (per serving): kcal 280 | pro 25g | carbs 15g | fat 12g

---

Avocado Power Wrap

Servings: 1 person

Prep Time: 15 minutes (including cooking)

Ingredients:
- 1 low-carb tortilla
- 2 scrambled eggs
- 1/4 avocado, sliced
- 1/2 cup fresh spinach
- Salt, to taste
- Pepper, to taste

Possible Variations:
You can add a few lean turkey slices for extra protein or swap the tortilla for large lettuce leaves if you prefer an even lighter option.twist.

Preparation:
1. Warm the low-carb tortilla in a skillet over medium heat for about 30 seconds on each side.
2. On the warmed tortilla, layer 1/2 cup fresh spinach.
3. Top with 2 scrambled eggs seasoned with salt and pepper.
4. Arrange 1/4 avocado slices over the eggs.
5. Roll the tortilla tightly into a wrap and serve immediately.

Nutritional Info (per serving): kcal 320 | pro 22g | carbs 10g | fat 20g

Cottage Crunch Sunrise Bowl

Servings: 1 bowl

Prep Time: 5 minutes

Ingredients:
- 1 cup low-fat cottage cheese
- 1/4 cup chopped walnuts
- 1/2 cup mixed fresh berries
- 1 teaspoon honey (optional)
- A pinch of cinnamon (optional)
- Fresh mint leaves (optional)

Possible Variations:
Feel free to substitute walnuts with almonds or pecans, and experiment with different berry combinations for a personalized twist.

Preparation:
1. In a bowl, combine 1 cup low-fat cottage cheese, 1/2 cup mixed fresh berries, and 1/4 cup chopped walnuts.
2. If desired, drizzle with 1 teaspoon honey and sprinkle a pinch of cinnamon over the mixture.
3. Garnish with fresh mint leaves and serve immediately.

Nutritional Info (per serving): kcal 250 | pro 28g | carbs 12g | fat 10g

---

Turkey Twist Scramble

Servings: 1 person

Prep Time: 15 minutes

Ingredients:
- 2 large eggs
- 2 oz lean turkey breast, diced
- 1/2 cup baby spinach
- 1/4 cup diced tomatoes
- Salt, to taste
- Pepper, to taste

Possible Variations:
You may add a sprinkle of low-fat cheese or swap tomatoes with diced bell peppers to vary the flavor.

Preparation:
1. In a non-stick skillet over medium heat, cook 2 oz diced lean turkey breast until lightly browned (about 3–4 minutes).
2. Add 1/2 cup baby spinach and 1/4 cup diced tomatoes; sauté for about 2 minutes until the spinach wilts.
3. Whisk 2 large eggs with salt and pepper, then pour them into the skillet.
4. Gently scramble everything together for 3–4 minutes until the eggs are fully cooked.
5. Serve immediately.

Nutritional Info (per serving): kcal 280 | pro 25g | carbs 7g | fat 16g

Chia Charge Overnight Pudding

Servings: 1 serving　　　　　　　　　　　**Prep Time:** 5 minutes (plus overnight chilling)

Ingredients:
- 1 cup unsweetened almond milk
- 3 tablespoons chia seeds
- 1 scoop vanilla protein powder
- 1/2 teaspoon vanilla extract
- A few fresh berries for topping
- Stevia or 1 teaspoon honey (optional)

Possible Variations:
Try using coconut milk instead of almond milk for a different flavor, or add a dash of cinnamon for extra spice.

Preparation:
1. In a jar, combine 1 cup unsweetened almond milk, 3 tablespoons chia seeds, 1 scoop vanilla protein powder, and 1/2 teaspoon vanilla extract; stir until well mixed.
2. Cover the jar and refrigerate overnight (or for at least 4 hours) until the mixture thickens into a pudding-like consistency.
3. In the morning, stir the pudding, top with a few fresh berries, and add stevia or honey if desired.
4. Serve chilled.

Nutritional Info (per serving): kcal 240 | pro 20g | carbs 12g | fat 12g

---

Turbo Breakfast Burrito

Servings: 1 burrito　　　　　　　　　　　**Prep Time:** 20 minutes

Ingredients:
- 1 low-carb tortilla
- 2 scrambled eggs
- 2 oz turkey sausage, sliced
- 1/4 cup shredded low-fat cheese
- 1/4 cup low-sugar salsa
- A handful of baby spinach

Possible Variations:
Consider adding diced avocado for extra creaminess or swapping turkey sausage with chicken sausage for a different flavor twist.

Preparation:
1. In a non-stick skillet, cook 2 oz sliced turkey sausage until lightly browned.
2. Add a handful of baby spinach and cook until wilted; then add 2 scrambled eggs seasoned with salt and pepper, stirring until just set.
3. On a low-carb tortilla, layer the turkey sausage and egg mixture, sprinkle 1/4 cup shredded low-fat cheese, and drizzle with 1/4 cup salsa.
4. Roll up the tortilla tightly into a burrito and, if desired, heat briefly in the skillet to melt the cheese further.
5. Serve warm.

Nutritional Info (per serving): kcal 310 | pro 22g | carbs 12g | fat 18g

Salmon Sizzle Toast

Servings: 1 person

Prep Time: 10 minutes

Ingredients:
- 1 slice low-carb bread
- 2 oz grilled fresh salmon (pre-cooked)
- 1/4 avocado, mashed
- 1 teaspoon lemon juice
- Salt, to taste
- Pepper, to taste

Possible Variations:
You can substitute fresh salmon with smoked salmon or add a sprinkle of capers or fresh dill for an extra burst of flavor.

Preparation:
1. Toast the low-carb bread until golden.
2. Spread the mashed avocado evenly over the toast.
3. Layer the grilled salmon on top.
4. Drizzle with lemon juice and season with salt and pepper.
5. Serve immediately.

Nutritional Info (per serving): kcal 280 | pro 18g | carbs 10g | fat 16g

Radiant Avocado Egg Bowl

Servings: 1 bowl

Prep Time: 15 minutes

Ingredients:
- 2 hard-boiled eggs, chopped
- 1/2 avocado, diced
- 1 cup arugula (or mixed greens)
- 1 teaspoon lime juice
- Salt, to taste
- Pepper, to taste

Possible Variations:
You can add a few cherry tomatoes for extra color or substitute arugula with spinach if preferred.

Preparation:
1. In a bowl, combine the chopped eggs, diced avocado, and arugula.
2. Drizzle with lime juice, and season with salt and pepper.
3. Toss gently until well mixed, then serve immediately.

Nutritional Info (per serving): kcal 270 | pro 18g | carbs 8g | fat 20g

Nutty Berry Dream Yogurt

Servings: 1 bowl

Prep Time: 5 minutes

Ingredients:
- 1 cup unsweetened almond yogurt
- 1/2 cup mixed berries
- 1 tablespoon chopped walnuts
- 1 teaspoon chia seeds
- 1 teaspoon honey (optional)
- A pinch of cinnamon (optional)

Preparation:
1. In a bowl, combine the almond yogurt, mixed berries, chopped walnuts, and chia seeds.
2. Optionally, drizzle with honey and sprinkle a pinch of cinnamon over the top.
3. Mix gently and serve immediately.

Possible Variations:
Feel free to substitute walnuts with almonds or pecans for a different nutty flavor.

Nutritional Info (per serving): kcal 240 | pro 15g | carbs 14g | fat 10g

---

Flash Protein Smoothie

Servings: 1 serving

Prep Time: 5 minutes

Ingredients:
- 1 cup unsweetened almond milk
- 1 scoop vanilla protein powder
- 1/2 cup frozen mixed berries
- 1/2 cup frozen spinach
- 1/4 avocado
- Ice cubes (optional)

Preparation:
1. Place all the ingredients into a blender.
2. Blend on high until the mixture is smooth and creamy.
3. Pour into a glass and serve immediately.

Possible Variations:
You can replace the frozen spinach with kale or add a few extra ice cubes for a thicker texture.

Nutritional Info (per serving): kcal 250 | pro 25g | carbs 15g | fat 8g

Dynamo Turkey Wrap

Servings: 1 wrap

Prep Time: 15 minutes

Ingredients:
- 1 low-carb tortilla
- 3 oz sliced lean turkey breast (pre-cooked)
- 1/4 avocado, sliced
- 1/2 cup mixed greens
- 1 tablespoon light mayonnaise or Greek yogurt
- Salt & pepper, to taste

Possible Variations:
You may add a few tomato slices for extra juiciness or swap turkey for chicken breast for a different flavor twist.

Preparation:
1. Lay the low-carb tortilla flat and spread the light mayonnaise or Greek yogurt evenly over it.
2. Layer the mixed greens, turkey slices, and avocado on top.
3. Season with salt and pepper.
4. Roll the tortilla tightly into a wrap and serve immediately.

Nutritional Info (per serving): kcal 310 | pro 26g | carbs 12g | fat 18g

---

Zesty Zoodle Spark Stir-Fry

Servings: 1 person

Prep Time: 20 minutes

Ingredients:
- 4 oz grilled chicken breast, sliced
- 1 medium zucchini, spiralized into noodles
- 1/2 cup cherry tomatoes, halved
- 1 tablespoon olive oil
- Salt, to taste
- Pepper, to taste

Possible Variations:
If you'd prefer seafood, you can substitute the chicken with 4 oz grilled shrimp for a different twist on this zoodle stir-fry.

Preparation:
1. Heat a non-stick skillet over medium heat and add 1 tablespoon olive oil.
2. Add all the ingredients to the skillet: the spiralized zucchini, cherry tomatoes, and sliced grilled chicken.
3. Sauté for about 3–4 minutes until the zucchini is tender but still crisp and the tomatoes soften slightly.
4. Season with salt and pepper, toss gently, and serve immediately.

Nutritional Info (per serving): kcal 300 | pro 28g | carbs 9g | fat 14g

Ricotta Radiance Pancakes

Servings: 1 serving (yields 3 small pancakes) **Prep Time:** 25 minutes

Ingredients:
- 1/2 cup low-fat ricotta cheese
- 1 large egg
- 1/4 cup almond flour
- 1/4 cup fresh blueberries
- A pinch of salt (optional)
- 1/2 teaspoon vanilla extract (optional)

Possible Variations:
You can substitute blueberries with raspberries or strawberries, or add a dash of cinnamon to the batter for a warming spice note.

Preparation:
1. In a bowl, whisk together the almond flour, low-fat ricotta, egg, and vanilla extract (if using) until you obtain a smooth batter.
2. Carefully fold in the fresh blueberries and a pinch of salt if desired.
3. Heat a non-stick skillet over medium heat and lightly coat it with cooking spray.
4. Spoon small rounds of the batter onto the skillet and cook for 3–4 minutes on each side until the pancakes are golden and set.
5. Remove from the skillet and serve warm.

Nutritional Info (per serving): kcal 290 | pro 18g | carbs 10g | fat 18g

Broccoli Boost Egg Muffins

Servings: 4 muffins **Prep Time:** 25 minutes (including baking)

Ingredients:
- 6 large eggs
- 1/2 cup finely chopped broccoli
- 1/4 cup shredded low-fat cheddar cheese
- Salt, to taste
- Pepper, to taste
- 1 teaspoon olive oil

Possible Variations:
For a different flavor, try swapping the cheddar with crumbled feta or substituting the broccoli with spinach or kale.

Preparation:
1. Preheat your oven to 350°F.
2. In a bowl, whisk together the eggs with salt and pepper, then stir in the chopped broccoli and shredded cheddar cheese along with 1 teaspoon olive oil.
3. Pour the mixture evenly into a greased muffin tin, filling each cup about 3/4 full.
4. Bake for 18–20 minutes until the muffins are set and lightly golden on top.
5. Remove from the oven, let cool slightly, and serve warm.

Nutritional Info (per muffin): kcal 80 | pro 7g | carbs 2g | fat 5g

Creamy Avocado Delight Salad

Servings: 1 bowl

Prep Time: 15 minutes

Ingredients:
- 2 hard-boiled eggs, chopped
- 1/2 avocado, diced
- 1 cup mixed greens
- 1 tablespoon lemon juice
- Salt, to taste
- Pepper, to taste

Preparation:
1. In a bowl, combine the chopped hard-boiled eggs, diced avocado, and mixed greens.
2. Drizzle with 1 tablespoon lemon juice and season with salt and pepper.
3. Toss gently to mix all the flavors, then serve immediately.

Possible Variations:
If you'd like a burst of extra color and flavor, add a few halved cherry tomatoes or a sprinkle of crumbled feta cheese to this salad.

Nutritional Info (per serving): kcal 270 | pro 18g | carbs 8g | fat 20g

Cottage Power Smoothie Supreme

Servings: 1 serving

Prep Time: 5 minutes

Ingredients:
- 1/2 cup low-fat cottage cheese
- 1 cup unsweetened almond milk
- 1/2 cup frozen mixed berries
- 1 teaspoon honey (optional)

Preparation:
1. Place all the ingredients into a blender.
2. Blend on high until the mixture is smooth and creamy.
3. Pour the smoothie into a glass and serve immediately.

Possible Variations:
You may substitute the mixed berries with strawberries or blueberries, or add a small handful of spinach for an extra nutrient boost while keeping the flavor vibrant.

Nutritional Info (per serving): kcal 250 | pro 25g | carbs 15g | fat 8g

SIMPLE AND SATISFYING LUNCHES

Nourishing Meals on the Go

Lunch is your midday opportunity to refuel with a dish that's both complete and satisfying, without demanding hours in the kitchen. In this category, you'll find recipes designed to be quick and easy, often incorporating pre-prepared ingredients like grilled chicken, boiled quinoa, or sautéed vegetables.

This approach gives you the freedom to create a flavorful, balanced meal in just minutes—no fuss, no stress. Enjoy wholesome, high-protein, low-carb lunches that keep you energized and satisfied, whether you're at home, at work, or on the move.

Zesty Garden Chicken Wrap

Servings: 1 person

Prep Time: 15 minutes (including assembly)

Ingredients:
- 1 low-carb tortilla
- 3 oz grilled chicken breast (sliced; pre-cooked)
- 1/2 cup shredded romaine lettuce
- 1/4 cup diced tomatoes
- 1 teaspoon lime juice
- Salt & pepper, to taste

Possible Variations:
If you like a creamier texture, try adding a tablespoon of Greek yogurt or a light tzatziki sauce. You can also experiment by tossing in some thinly sliced red onions or swapping the tortilla for large lettuce leaves for a lower-carb option.

Preparation:
1. Warm the low-carb tortilla in a dry skillet over medium heat for about 30 seconds on each side.
2. Lay the tortilla flat and evenly spread the shredded lettuce over it.
3. Place the sliced, pre-cooked grilled chicken and diced tomatoes on top.
4. Drizzle with 1 teaspoon lime juice, then season with salt and pepper.
5. Roll the tortilla tightly into a wrap, cut in half if desired, and serve immediately.

Nutritional Info (per serving): kcal 320 | pro 28g | carbs 10g | fat 16g

---

Avocado & Turkey Power Bowl

Servings: 1 bowl

Prep Time: 15 minutes

Ingredients:
- 3 oz sliced lean turkey breast (pre-cooked)
- 1/2 avocado, diced
- 1/2 cup mixed greens
- 1/4 cup cherry tomatoes, halved
- 1 tablespoon olive oil
- 1 teaspoon apple cider vinegar

Possible Variations:
For an extra flavor twist, try adding a sprinkle of crumbled feta cheese or a handful of sliced cucumbers. You could also swap the apple cider vinegar with lemon juice for a different tang.

Preparation:
1. In a bowl, combine the mixed greens, pre-cooked turkey slices, diced avocado, and cherry tomatoes.
2. Drizzle with 1 tablespoon olive oil and 1 teaspoon apple cider vinegar.
3. Toss gently to ensure all ingredients are evenly coated.
4. Season with salt and pepper if desired, then serve immediately.

Nutritional Info (per serving): kcal 310 | pro 26g | carbs 12g | fat 18g

Citrus Salmon Salad Sizzle

Servings: 1 bowl

Prep Time: 15 minutes

Ingredients:
- 4 oz grilled salmon (pre-cooked)
- 2 cups mixed greens
- 1/2 cup cucumber slices
- 1 tablespoon olive oil
- 1 tablespoon lemon juice
- Salt & pepper, to taste

Possible Variations:
For a twist, try substituting grilled salmon with trout or another white fish, and consider adding a few slices of avocado for extra creaminess.

Preparation:
1. In a bowl, combine the mixed greens and cucumber slices.
2. Top with the pre-cooked grilled salmon.
3. Drizzle with 1 tablespoon olive oil and 1 tablespoon lemon juice.
4. Season with salt and pepper, toss gently, and serve immediately.

Nutritional Info (per serving): kcal 360 | pro 32g | carbs 8g | fat 20g

Quinoa & Veggie Boost Bowl

Servings: 4 bowl

Prep Time: 25 minutes

Ingredients:
- 1/2 cup cooked quinoa (pre-cooked)
- 1/2 cup steamed broccoli florets
- 1/4 cup diced red bell pepper
- 1/4 cup chopped cucumber
- 1 tablespoon olive oil
- 1 tablespoon lemon juice

Possible Variations:
If you're looking to reduce carbs further, you can substitute quinoa with cauliflower rice. Alternatively, add a dash of your favorite herbs (such as parsley or cilantro) for an extra burst of flavor.

Preparation:
1. In a bowl, combine the pre-cooked quinoa, steamed broccoli, diced red bell pepper, and chopped cucumber.
2. Drizzle with 1 tablespoon olive oil and 1 tablespoon lemon juice.
3. Toss the ingredients together until well mixed, then season with salt and pepper if desired.
4. Serve warm or chilled as preferred.

Nutritional Info (per serving): kcal 350 | pro 28g | carbs 20g | fat 12g

Spicy Shrimp Lunch Delight

Servings: 1 bowl

Prep Time: 20 minutes

Ingredients:
- 4 oz grilled shrimp (pre-cooked)
- 1 cup mixed greens
- 1/4 cup diced red bell pepper
- 1 tablespoon low-sodium soy sauce
- 1/2 teaspoon sriracha sauce
- Salt, to taste

Possible Variations:
If you prefer a milder flavor, reduce the sriracha or omit it altogether, and consider adding a squeeze of fresh lime juice for extra zest. You might also swap shrimp with grilled scallops for a luxurious change.

Preparation:
1. In a bowl, combine the mixed greens, diced red bell pepper, and pre-cooked grilled shrimp.
2. Drizzle with 1 tablespoon low-sodium soy sauce and 1/2 teaspoon sriracha sauce.
3. Toss everything together until well coated; adjust salt if necessary.
4. Serve immediately.

Nutritional Info (per serving): kcal 330 | pro 28g | carbs 10g | fat 15g

---

Lean Beef Crunch Salad

Servings: 1 person

Prep Time: 20 minutes (including cooking)

Ingredients:
- 4 oz lean beef strips (pre-cooked, grilled or pan-seared)
- 2 cups mixed greens
- 1/2 cup shredded carrots
- 1/4 cup diced cucumber
- 1 tablespoon olive oil
- 1 tablespoon balsamic vinegar

Possible Variations:
You might add a handful of toasted pine nuts for extra crunch, swap balsamic vinegar for red wine vinegar, or include thinly sliced radishes for a peppery bite.

Preparation:
1. In a bowl, combine the mixed greens, shredded carrots, and diced cucumber.
2. Slice the pre-cooked beef strips if needed, and add them to the bowl.
3. Drizzle with olive oil and balsamic vinegar.
4. Toss gently until all ingredients are evenly coated.
5. Season with salt and pepper to taste, then serve immediately.

Nutritional Info (per serving): kcal 340 | pro 27g | carbs 10g | fat 17g

Mediterranean Chicken Wrap

Servings: 1 wrap

Prep Time: 15 minutes (including assembly)

Ingredients:
- 1 low-carb tortilla
- 3 oz grilled chicken breast (sliced; pre-cooked)
- 1 tablespoon hummus
- 1/4 cup diced cucumber
- 1/4 cup chopped romaine lettuce
- 1 teaspoon olive oil

Possible Variations:
For an extra creamy texture, try adding a few thin slices of avocado or swap the hummus for a light tzatziki sauce for a refreshing Mediterranean twist.

Preparation:
1. Warm the low-carb tortilla in a dry skillet over medium heat for about 30 seconds on each side.
2. Spread the hummus evenly over the tortilla.
3. Layer on the pre-cooked, sliced chicken breast, diced cucumber, and chopped romaine lettuce.
4. Drizzle with olive oil, then roll the tortilla tightly into a wrap.
5. Serve immediately.

Nutritional Info (per serving): kcal 330 | pro 28g | carbs 12g | fat 15g

Tuna Tango Lettuce Boats

Servings: 1 (yield: 2 lettuce boats)

Prep Time: 15 minutes

Ingredients:
- 1 can tuna in water (drained)
- 1 tablespoon plain Greek yogurt
- 1 teaspoon Dijon mustard
- Salt & pepper, to taste
- 2 large butter lettuce leaves
- 1 tablespoon diced celery

Possible Variations:
Enhance the flavor with a squeeze of lemon juice or a few capers, or substitute the butter lettuce with romaine leaves for a crunchier texture.

Preparation:
1. In a bowl, mix the tuna with Greek yogurt, Dijon mustard, salt, and pepper (and diced celery if you choose to add it).
2. Spoon the mixture evenly into the two butter lettuce leaves to form "boats."
3. Serve immediately.

Nutritional Info (per serving): kcal 280 | pro 25g | carbs 5g | fat 18g

Greek Power Chicken Salad

Servings: 1 bowl | **Prep Time:** 15 minutes

Ingredients:
- 3 oz grilled chicken breast (sliced; pre-cooked)
- 1 cup chopped romaine lettuce
- 1/4 cup diced cucumber
- 1/4 cup halved cherry tomatoes
- 2 tablespoons plain Greek yogurt
- 1 teaspoon olive oil

Possible Variations:
For added flavor, mix in a few kalamata olives or a sprinkle of crumbled feta cheese, or replace the Greek yogurt with a light lemon-dill dressing for a tangier taste.

Preparation:
1. In a bowl, combine the chopped romaine lettuce, diced cucumber, and halved cherry tomatoes.
2. Top with the sliced, pre-cooked grilled chicken breast.
3. Drizzle the Greek yogurt and olive oil over the salad.
4. Toss gently until all ingredients are evenly coated, then serve immediately.

Nutritional Info (per serving): kcal 320 | pro 30g | carbs 10g | fat 14g

---

Crispy Tofu & Kale Fiesta

Servings: 1 bowl | **Prep Time:** 25 minutes

Ingredients:
- 4 oz firm tofu (cubed)
- 1 cup chopped kale
- 1/2 red bell pepper (sliced)
- 1 tablespoon low-sodium soy sauce
- 1 teaspoon sesame oil
- 1 teaspoon sesame seeds

Possible Variations:
For a different texture, you can substitute tofu with tempeh. Additionally, you may add a dash of chili flakes for extra spice or swap kale with spinach if you prefer a milder flavor.

Preparation:
1. Heat the sesame oil in a non-stick skillet over medium-high heat.
2. Add the cubed tofu and stir-fry until it becomes lightly crispy, about 4–5 minutes.
3. Add the chopped kale and sliced red bell pepper, and continue stir-frying for another 3–4 minutes until the kale is slightly wilted and the bell pepper softens.
4. Drizzle with soy sauce, sprinkle with sesame seeds, toss gently, and serve immediately.

Nutritional Info (per serving): kcal 320 | pro 20g | carbs 10g | fat 18g

Ultimate Turkey Cobb Wrap

Servings: 1 wrap

Prep Time: 20 minutes

Ingredients:
- 1 low-carb tortilla
- 3 oz sliced lean turkey breast (pre-cooked)
- 1 hard-boiled egg, sliced
- 1/4 avocado, sliced
- 1 cup mixed greens
- 1 tablespoon light vinaigrette

Possible Variations:
If you desire an extra burst of flavor, you can add thin slices of tomato or a sprinkle of crumbled feta cheese. Alternatively, swap the turkey breast for grilled chicken for a different twist on this hearty wrap.

Preparation:
1. Warm the low-carb tortilla in a dry skillet over medium heat for about 30 seconds on each side.
2. Lay the tortilla flat and spread the mixed greens evenly over it.
3. Arrange the pre-cooked turkey breast slices, followed by the sliced hard-boiled egg and avocado.
4. Drizzle with 1 tablespoon of light vinaigrette.
5. Roll the tortilla tightly into a wrap and serve immediately.

Nutritional Info (per serving): kcal 350 | pro 30g | carbs 12g | fat 18g

---

Sassy Egg & Avocado Salad

Servings: 1 bowl

Prep Time: 15 minutes

Ingredients:
- 2 hard-boiled eggs, chopped
- 1/2 avocado, diced
- 1 cup mixed greens
- 1 tablespoon lemon juice
- Salt, to taste
- Pepper, to taste

Possible Variations:
You may add a handful of cherry tomatoes or finely chopped red onion for additional zest, or even a light sprinkle of your favorite herbs to enhance the flavor further.

Preparation:
1. In a bowl, combine the chopped hard-boiled eggs, diced avocado, and mixed greens.
2. Drizzle with 1 tablespoon of lemon juice and season with salt and pepper.
3. Toss gently to mix all the flavors and serve immediately.

Nutritional Info (per serving): kcal 270 | pro 18g | carbs 8g | fat 20g

Herb-Infused Chicken Zoodle Salad

Servings: 1 bowl

Prep Time: 20 minutes

Ingredients:
- 4 oz grilled chicken breast (sliced; pre-cooked)
- 1 medium zucchini, spiralized into noodles
- 1/2 cup cherry tomatoes, halved
- 1 tablespoon olive oil
- Fresh basil, chopped
- Salt & pepper, to taste

Possible Variations:
For a seafood twist, substitute the chicken with 4 oz grilled shrimp. You can also experiment by adding a squeeze of lemon juice to brighten the flavors even more.

Preparation:
1. In a bowl, combine the spiralized zucchini noodles and halved cherry tomatoes.
2. Add the sliced, pre-cooked grilled chicken breast on top.
3. Drizzle with 1 tablespoon olive oil and sprinkle with freshly chopped basil.
4. Season with salt and pepper, toss gently, and serve immediately.

Nutritional Info (per serving): kcal 300 | pro 28g | carbs 9g | fat 14g

Refreshing Shrimp & Cucumber Bowl

Servings: 1 bowl

Prep Time: 15 minutes

Ingredients:
- 4 oz grilled shrimp (pre-cooked)
- 1/2 cup diced cucumber
- 1/2 cup halved cherry tomatoes
- 1 cup mixed greens
- 1 tablespoon olive oil
- 1 tablespoon lemon juice

Possible Variations:
If you prefer, swap the shrimp with grilled scallops or chicken for a change. Adding a few sliced radishes can also give the salad an extra crunch and a peppery note.

Preparation:
1. In a bowl, combine the mixed greens, diced cucumber, and halved cherry tomatoes.
2. Top the salad with the pre-cooked grilled shrimp.
3. Drizzle with 1 tablespoon olive oil and 1 tablespoon lemon juice.
4. Toss gently, season with salt and pepper if desired, and serve immediately.

Nutritional Info (per serving): kcal 320 | pro 26g | carbs 10g | fat 16g

Lean Turkey & Spinach Power Wrap

Servings: 1 wrap

Prep Time: 15 minutes

Ingredients:
- 1 low-carb tortilla
- 3 oz sliced lean turkey breast (pre-cooked)
- 1/2 cup fresh spinach
- 1/4 avocado, sliced
- 1 tablespoon light mayonnaise or plain Greek yogurt
- Salt & pepper, to taste

Possible Variations:
You can swap the turkey breast for grilled chicken if desired, or add a few slices of tomato for extra juiciness. Enjoy customizing this power wrap to suit your taste!

Preparation:
1. Warm the low-carb tortilla in a skillet over medium heat for about 30 seconds on each side.
2. Spread 1 tablespoon of light mayonnaise or Greek yogurt evenly over the tortilla.
3. Layer with 1/2 cup fresh spinach, pre-cooked turkey breast slices, and 1/4 avocado slices.
4. Season with salt and pepper, then roll the tortilla tightly into a wrap.
5. Serve immediately.

Nutritional Info (per serving): kcal 310 | pro 26g | carbs 12g | fat 18g

---

Hearty Quinoa Veggie Wrap

Servings: 1 wrap

Prep Time: 20 minutes

Ingredients:
- 1 low-carb tortilla
- 1/2 cup cooked quinoa (pre-cooked)
- 1/2 cup mixed greens
- 1/4 cup shredded carrots
- 1 tablespoon hummus
- Salt & pepper, to taste

Possible Variations:
You can add diced cucumber for extra crunch or swap the hummus with a light tzatziki sauce for a refreshing twist.

Preparation:
1. Warm the low-carb tortilla in a dry skillet over medium heat for about 30 seconds on each side.
2. On the warmed tortilla, spread 1 tablespoon of hummus evenly over the surface.
3. Add the pre-cooked quinoa, mixed greens, and shredded carrots on top.
4. Season with salt and pepper, then roll the tortilla tightly into a wrap.
5. Serve immediately.

Nutritional Info (per serving): kcal 320 | pro 20g | carbs 18g | fat 12g

Spicy Chicken Caesar Lettuce Cups

Servings: 1 (yield: 2 lettuce cups) **Prep Time:** 15 minutes

Ingredients:
- 2 large romaine lettuce leaves
- 3 oz grilled chicken breast (sliced; pre-cooked)
- 1 tablespoon light Caesar dressing
- 1 tablespoon grated Parmesan cheese
- 1/4 teaspoon crushed red pepper flakes
- Salt & pepper, to taste

Possible Variations:
For a milder flavor, reduce or omit the red pepper flakes; you can also add a few capers or substitute Caesar dressing with a lemon-Dijon vinaigrette.

Preparation:
1. Rinse and pat dry the romaine lettuce leaves, then arrange them on a plate to serve as cups.
2. Distribute the pre-cooked, sliced chicken breast evenly between the lettuce leaves.
3. Drizzle with 1 tablespoon of light Caesar dressing and sprinkle grated Parmesan cheese over the top.
4. Add 1/4 teaspoon crushed red pepper flakes, and season with salt and pepper as desired.
5. Serve immediately.

Nutritional Info (per serving): kcal 300 | pro 25g | carbs 5g | fat 15g

Protein-Packed Mediterranean Salad

Servings: 1 bowl **Prep Time:** 15 minutes

Ingredients:
- 3 oz grilled chicken breast (sliced; pre-cooked)
- 1 cup mixed greens
- 1/4 cup diced cucumber
- 1/4 cup halved cherry tomatoes
- 1 tablespoon olive oil
- 1 tablespoon red wine vinegar
- Salt & pepper, to taste

Possible Variations:
For extra Mediterranean flavor, add a handful of olives or a sprinkle of crumbled feta cheese.

Preparation:
1. In a bowl, combine the mixed greens, diced cucumber, and halved cherry tomatoes.
2. Top with the sliced, pre-cooked grilled chicken breast.
3. Drizzle 1 tablespoon of olive oil and 1 tablespoon of red wine vinegar over the salad.
4. Toss gently until evenly coated, then season with salt and pepper.
5. Serve immediately.

Nutritional Info (per serving): kcal 320 | pro 30g | carbs 10g | fat 14g

Vibrant Veggie & Tuna Power Pack

Servings: 1 bowl   **Prep Time:** 15 minutes

Ingredients:
- 1 can tuna in water (drained)
- 1/2 cup mixed greens
- 1/4 cup diced cucumber
- 1/4 cup halved cherry tomatoes
- 1 tablespoon plain Greek yogurt
- Salt & pepper, to taste

Possible Variations:
For an extra burst of flavor, try adding diced celery or substitute the Greek yogurt with mashed avocado for a creamier texture.

Preparation:
1. In a bowl, combine the mixed greens, diced cucumber, and halved cherry tomatoes.
2. Add the drained tuna and 1 tablespoon of plain Greek yogurt to the bowl.
3. Mix thoroughly until all the ingredients are well incorporated.
4. Season with salt and pepper to taste, then serve immediately.

Nutritional Info (per serving): kcal 310 | pro 25g | carbs 9g | fat 16g

---

Fresh & Zesty Turkey Wrap Supreme

Servings: 1 wrap   **Prep Time:** 15 minutes

Ingredients:
- 1 low-carb tortilla
- 3 oz sliced lean turkey breast (pre-cooked)
- 1/4 avocado, sliced
- 1/4 cup shredded romaine lettuce
- 1 tablespoon light vinaigrette
- Salt & pepper, to taste

Possible Variations:
You may add a few tomato slices for extra juiciness or swap the light vinaigrette with a mustard-based dressing for a different flavor profile.

Preparation:
1. Warm the low-carb tortilla in a dry skillet over medium heat for about 30 seconds on each side.
2. Spread 1 tablespoon of light vinaigrette evenly over the tortilla.
3. Layer with the shredded romaine lettuce, pre-cooked turkey breast slices, and avocado slices.
4. Season with salt and pepper, then roll the tortilla tightly into a wrap.
5. Serve immediately.

Nutritional Info (per serving): kcal 310 | pro 26g | carbs 12g | fat 18g

DINNERS READY IN NO TIME

Wholesome Meals for Busy Evenings

After a long day, you deserve a dinner that's both nourishing and delicious—without spending hours in the kitchen. In this category, you'll find recipes designed to be ready in 30 minutes or less, so you can enjoy a satisfying, high-protein, low-carb meal even on your busiest nights.

These recipes are perfect for the whole family, making it easy to create healthy eating habits without anyone even noticing the change—thanks to their super tasty flavors that everyone will love. Many dishes incorporate pre-cooked ingredients like grilled chicken or steamed veggies, allowing you to quickly assemble a complete, balanced dinner that not only refuels your body but also brings the family together around the table.

When it comes to dinner, these recipes are designed with your busy life in mind. They rely on pre-cooked ingredients—like grilled chicken, steamed vegetables, and pre-made quinoa or cauliflower rice—to help you quickly assemble a nourishing, high-protein, low-carb meal after a hectic day. For those who come home after work or juggle a fast-paced schedule, dedicating one day a week to batch-cooking essential ingredients is a perfect shortcut.

This approach not only saves you time but also makes it easier to stick to your healthy eating goals, ensuring that every dinner is both delicious and stress-free for the whole family.

Get ready to discover quick, creative, and flavorful recipes that help you wind down, refuel, and effortlessly build lasting, healthy habits for everyone.

Zesty Lemon Chicken Express

Servings: 1 person

Prep Time: 25 minutes (including cooking)

Ingredients:
- 4 oz chicken breast (pre-cooked, grilled or pan-seared)
- 1 tablespoon olive oil
- 1 tablespoon lemon juice
- 1/2 cup broccoli florets (steamed or quickly sautéed)
- Salt, to taste
- Pepper, to taste

Possible Variations:
If you prefer a creamier twist, try adding a tablespoon of plain Greek yogurt at the end. You may also swap broccoli with asparagus or green beans for a different texture.

Preparation:
1. Heat the olive oil in a non-stick skillet over medium heat.
2. Add the pre-cooked chicken breast (sliced if desired) along with the broccoli florets, and warm for about 3–4 minutes.
3. Drizzle with lemon juice and season with salt and pepper.
4. Toss gently to combine all flavors and serve immediately.

Nutritional Info (per serving): kcal 340 | pro 26g | carbs 12g | fat 16g

Garlic Herb Salmon Surprise

Servings: 1 person

Prep Time: 20 minutes (including cooking)

Ingredients:
- 4 oz grilled salmon (pre-cooked)
- 1 tablespoon olive oil
- 1 clove garlic, minced
- 1 tablespoon lemon juice
- 1/2 cup steamed asparagus
- Salt & pepper, to taste

Possible Variations:
You can substitute asparagus with steamed green beans or broccoli. Adding a sprinkle of fresh dill or parsley before serving also enhances the herbal note.

Preparation:
1. Warm the pre-cooked salmon and steamed asparagus gently in a non-stick skillet over medium heat with olive oil for about 3–4 minutes.
2. Stir in the minced garlic and lemon juice, and season with salt and pepper.
3. Allow the flavors to meld for an additional minute, then serve immediately.

Nutritional Info (per serving): kcal 360 | pro 32g | carbs 8g | fat 20g

Spicy Shrimp & Broccoli Blitz

Servings: 1 person

Prep Time: 20 minutes

Ingredients:
- 4 oz grilled shrimp (pre-cooked)
- 1 cup broccoli florets (steamed or quickly sautéed)
- 1 tablespoon olive oil
- 1/2 teaspoon sriracha sauce
- 1 teaspoon lemon juice
- Salt & pepper, to taste

Preparation:
1. In a skillet over medium heat, combine the pre-cooked shrimp and broccoli florets with olive oil.
2. Drizzle with sriracha sauce and lemon juice, and season with salt and pepper.
3. Stir-fry for about 3–4 minutes until everything is heated through and well combined.
4. Serve immediately.

Possible Variations:
For a milder flavor, reduce the sriracha or omit it altogether, and add a dash of fresh lime juice instead. You can also swap shrimp with grilled scallops for a luxurious change.

Nutritional Info (per serving): kcal 330 | pro 28g | carbs 10g | fat 15g

Crispy Chicken Veggie Skillet

Servings: 1 person

Prep Time: 25 minutes

Ingredients:
- 4 oz chicken breast (pre-cooked, sliced)
- 1/2 cup bell pepper strips
- 1/2 cup zucchini slices
- 1 tablespoon olive oil
- Salt, to taste
- Pepper, to taste

Preparation:
1. Heat the olive oil in a non-stick skillet over medium heat.
2. Add the pre-cooked, sliced chicken along with the bell pepper strips and zucchini slices.
3. Sauté for about 4–5 minutes until the vegetables are tender and slightly crispy.
4. Season with salt and pepper, toss well, and serve immediately.

Possible Variations:
Try adding a squeeze of lemon for brightness or swapping zucchini with yellow squash. You may also include a sprinkle of garlic powder for an extra flavor boost.

Nutritional Info (per serving): kcal 340 | pro 26g | carbs 12g | fat 16g

Teriyaki Turkey Stir-Fry

Servings: 1 person

Prep Time: 20 minutes

Ingredients:
- 4 oz lean turkey breast (sliced, pre-cooked)
- 1/2 cup snap peas
- 1/2 red bell pepper, sliced
- 1 tablespoon low-sodium teriyaki sauce
- 1 teaspoon olive oil
- Salt & pepper, to taste

Possible Variations:
You may substitute turkey with chicken breast for a different flavor, or add a sprinkle of sesame seeds for extra crunch. Enjoy customizing your stir-fry with your favorite veggies!

Preparation:
1. In a skillet over medium-high heat, warm the olive oil and add the pre-cooked turkey breast slices.
2. Toss in the snap peas and red bell pepper slices; stir-fry for about 4–5 minutes until the vegetables are tender but still crisp.
3. Drizzle with teriyaki sauce, season with salt and pepper, and toss to combine well.
4. Serve immediately.

Nutritional Info (per serving): kcal 330 | pro 28g | carbs 10g | fat 15g

Basil Lime Beef Quick-Bake

Servings: 1 person

Prep Time: 25 minutes (including cooking)

Ingredients:
- 4 oz lean beef strips
- 1 tablespoon olive oil
- 1 tablespoon lime juice
- 1/4 cup fresh basil, chopped
- Salt, to taste
- Pepper, to taste

Possible Variations:
For an extra flavor boost, try adding a dash of garlic powder or substitute lime juice with lemon juice for a slightly different citrus note.

Preparation:
1. Preheat your oven to 400°F.
2. In a bowl, combine all the ingredients by tossing the beef strips with olive oil, lime juice, fresh basil, salt, and pepper.
3. Spread the beef evenly on a baking sheet and bake for 10–12 minutes until cooked to your desired doneness.
4. Remove from the oven, let rest briefly, and serve immediately.

Nutritional Info (per serving): kcal 360 | pro 30g | carbs 4g | fat 18g

Cauliflower Rice Chicken Bowl

Servings: 1 bowl **Prep Time:** 25 minutes

Ingredients:
- 1 cup cauliflower rice (pre-cooked)
- 4 oz grilled chicken breast, sliced (pre-cooked)
- 1/2 cup steamed broccoli florets
- 1 tablespoon olive oil
- 1 tablespoon low-sodium soy sauce
- Salt & pepper, to taste

Possible Variations:
For a different twist, swap broccoli with snap peas or drizzle a little fresh lemon juice over the bowl before serving.

Preparation:
1. In a skillet over medium heat, warm the cauliflower rice with olive oil and low-sodium soy sauce for about 2–3 minutes.
2. Add the pre-cooked, sliced chicken breast and steamed broccoli florets to the skillet and heat through for an additional 2–3 minutes.
3. Season with salt and pepper, toss well, and serve immediately.

Nutritional Info (per serving): kcal 340 | pro 26g | carbs 10g | fat 12g

---

Rapid Pesto Zoodle Chicken

Servings: 1 bowl **Prep Time:** 20 minutes

Ingredients:
- 4 oz grilled chicken breast, sliced (pre-cooked)
- 1 medium zucchini, spiralized into noodles
- 1/2 cup cherry tomatoes, halved
- 2 tablespoons low-carb pesto
- Salt & pepper, to taste

Possible Variations:
For a different flavor profile, you can substitute the pesto with a homemade basil-lime dressing or add extra fresh basil leaves.

Preparation:
1. In a bowl, combine the spiralized zucchini noodles and halved cherry tomatoes.
2. Add the pre-cooked, sliced chicken breast to the bowl.
3. Drizzle 2 tablespoons of low-carb pesto over the ingredients and toss gently until well mixed.
4. Season with salt and pepper, then serve immediately.

Nutritional Info (per serving): kcal 300 | pro 28g | carbs 9g | fat 14g

Sizzling Steak & Pepper Medley

Servings: 1 bowl   **Prep Time:** 25 minutes

Ingredients:
- 4 oz lean steak, sliced (pre-cooked or quickly seared)
- 1/2 cup red bell pepper, sliced
- 1/2 cup yellow bell pepper, sliced
- 1 tablespoon olive oil
- Salt, to taste
- Pepper, to taste

Possible Variations:
Enhance the dish by adding a dash of Worcestershire sauce during cooking, or garnish with fresh parsley before serving for an extra burst of flavor.

Preparation:
1. If the steak is raw, quickly sear it in a skillet over medium-high heat with olive oil for about 3–4 minutes per side until medium-rare; if pre-cooked, warm the steak in the skillet for 1–2 minutes.
2. Add the sliced red and yellow bell peppers to the skillet and sauté for 4–5 minutes until the peppers are tender.
3. Toss the steak with the peppers, season with salt and pepper, and serve immediately.

Nutritional Info (per serving): kcal 360 | pro 30g | carbs 8g | fat 18g

---

Mediterranean Chicken Fiesta

Servings: 1 bowl   **Prep Time:** 25 minutes

Ingredients:
- 4 oz grilled chicken breast, sliced (pre-cooked)
- 1 cup mixed greens
- 1/4 cup diced cucumber
- 1/4 cup halved cherry tomatoes
- 1 tablespoon olive oil
- 1 tablespoon red wine vinegar

Possible Variations:
For an extra Mediterranean twist, consider adding a handful of Kalamata olives or a sprinkle of crumbled feta cheese.

Preparation:
1. In a bowl, combine the mixed greens, diced cucumber, and halved cherry tomatoes.
2. Top the salad with the pre-cooked, sliced chicken breast.
3. Drizzle with olive oil and red wine vinegar, then toss gently until all ingredients are evenly coated.
4. Serve immediately.

Nutritional Info (per serving): kcal 320 | pro 30g | carbs 10g | fat 14g

Homestyle Turkey Veggie Roast

Servings: 1 bowl

Prep Time: 30 minutes

Ingredients:
- 4 oz lean turkey breast (pre-cooked, sliced)
- 1 cup mixed roasted vegetables (carrots, zucchini, red bell pepper; pre-roasted)
- 1 tablespoon olive oil
- 1/2 teaspoon dried rosemary
- Salt, to taste
- Pepper, to taste

Possible Variations:
For a twist, you can swap the turkey for grilled chicken or replace rosemary with thyme for a different herbal note.

Preparation:
1. Preheat your oven to 400°F.
2. In a bowl, combine the pre-cooked turkey breast slices and the pre-roasted vegetables with the olive oil, dried rosemary, salt, and pepper.
3. Spread the mixture evenly on a baking sheet and bake for 10–12 minutes until everything is heated through.
4. Remove from the oven, toss gently, and serve immediately.

Nutritional Info (per serving): kcal 340 | pro 28g | carbs 12g | fat 16g

Speedy Tofu & Veggie Curry

Servings: 1 bowl

Prep Time: 30 minutes

Ingredients:
- 4 oz firm tofu (cubed)
- 1/2 cup mixed vegetables (such as broccoli florets and red bell pepper, roughly chopped)
- 1/2 cup fresh spinach
- 1 tablespoon unsweetened coconut milk
- 1 teaspoon curry powder
- Salt, to taste

Possible Variations:
You can add a squeeze of lime juice at the end for extra brightness or substitute tofu with tempeh for a firmer texture.

Preparation:
1. In a non-stick skillet, heat a little oil over medium heat and add the tofu cubes; sauté until they begin to brown, about 4 minutes.
2. Add all the mixed vegetables and fresh spinach to the skillet, then sprinkle in the curry powder; stir-fry for about 5 minutes until the vegetables are tender.
3. Pour in the unsweetened coconut milk and simmer for an additional 3 minutes, allowing the flavors to meld.
4. Season with salt, then serve immediately.

Nutritional Info (per serving): kcal 320 | pro 20g | carbs 10g | fat 18g

Flash-Fried Beef & Broccoli

Servings: 1 bowl

Prep Time: 25 minutes

Ingredients:
- 4 oz lean beef strips (raw or pre-cooked)
- 1 cup broccoli florets (steamed or quickly stir-fried)
- 1 tablespoon olive oil
- 1 tablespoon low-sodium soy sauce
- Salt, to taste
- Pepper, to taste

Possible Variations:
For an extra kick, add a minced garlic clove during cooking or substitute beef with lean chicken breast for a lighter option.

Preparation:
1. If using raw beef, heat olive oil in a skillet over medium-high heat and sear the beef strips for 3–4 minutes per side until medium-rare; if using pre-cooked beef, simply warm it in the skillet for 1–2 minutes.
2. Add the broccoli florets and stir-fry for an additional 4–5 minutes until tender and heated through.
3. Drizzle with low-sodium soy sauce, season with salt and pepper, toss well, and serve immediately.

Nutritional Info (per serving): kcal 360 | pro 30g | carbs 8g | fat 18g

---

Hearty Chicken Caesar Bake

Servings: 1 bowl

Prep Time: 30 minutes

Ingredients:
- 4 oz grilled chicken breast (sliced; pre-cooked)
- 1 cup chopped romaine lettuce
- 1/4 cup shredded low-fat Parmesan cheese
- 1 tablespoon light Caesar dressing
- Salt, to taste
- Pepper, to taste

Possible Variations:
For a zesty twist, add a squeeze of lemon juice before baking or substitute the romaine with fresh spinach.

Preparation:
1. Preheat your oven to 375°F.
2. In a baking dish, combine the chopped romaine lettuce and pre-cooked, sliced chicken breast with the light Caesar dressing.
3. Evenly sprinkle the shredded low-fat Parmesan cheese over the top and season with salt and pepper.
4. Bake for 10–12 minutes until the cheese is lightly melted and the dish is heated through.
5. Serve warm immediately.

Nutritional Info (per serving): kcal 340 | pro 30g | carbs 10g | fat 16g

Instant Avocado Lime Cod

Servings: 1 person

Prep Time: 25 minutes

Ingredients:
- 4 oz cod fillet (raw or pre-cooked)
- 1/4 avocado, diced
- 1 tablespoon olive oil
- 1 tablespoon lime juice
- Salt, to taste
- Pepper, to taste

Possible Variations:
You can substitute cod with another white fish like halibut or snapper, or add a sprinkle of chopped cilantro for an extra burst of freshness.

Preparation:
1. If the cod is raw, preheat your oven to 400°F, then season the cod fillet with salt and pepper, drizzle with olive oil and lime juice, and bake for 10–12 minutes until the fish is opaque and flakes easily; if pre-cooked, simply warm the cod in a skillet over medium heat for 3–4 minutes.
2. Top the cod with the diced avocado and serve immediately.

Nutritional Info (per serving): kcal 320 | pro 28g | carbs 8g | fat 18g

Family Fiesta Shrimp Tacos

Servings: 1 person

Prep Time: 20 minutes

Ingredients:
- 4 oz grilled shrimp (pre-cooked)
- 2 low-carb tortillas
- 1/4 cup shredded cabbage
- 1/4 cup diced tomatoes
- 1 tablespoon lime juice
- Salt, to taste

Possible Variations:
If you prefer a creamier texture, you can add a tablespoon of Greek yogurt or a light avocado crema to the mix. You might also experiment with different crunchy slaws by using shredded radishes or a blend of red and green cabbage.

Preparation:
1. Warm the 2 low-carb tortillas in a dry skillet over medium heat for about 30 seconds on each side.
2. In a bowl, combine the shredded cabbage and diced tomatoes with 1 tablespoon of lime juice and a pinch of salt.
3. Evenly distribute the pre-cooked shrimp among the tortillas and top with the cabbage-tomato mixture.
4. Roll each tortilla tightly into a taco and serve immediately.

Nutritional Info (per serving): kcal 350 | pro 28g | carbs 15g | fat 10g

Chili Lime Chicken Fajitas

Servings: 1 person

Prep Time: 20 minutes

Ingredients:
- 4 oz grilled chicken breast (sliced; pre-cooked)
- 1/2 cup bell pepper strips
- 1/4 cup sliced onions
- 1 tablespoon olive oil
- 1 tablespoon lime juice
- 1/2 teaspoon chili powder

Possible Variations:
For a milder version, reduce the chili powder or omit it entirely, then finish with extra lime juice. Alternatively, swap the chicken with turkey strips for a slightly different flavor profile.

Preparation:
1. Heat a skillet over medium-high heat and add 1 tablespoon of olive oil.
2. Add the bell pepper strips and sliced onions to the skillet and sauté for about 4–5 minutes until they become tender-crisp.
3. Stir in the pre-cooked, sliced chicken breast and sprinkle with 1/2 teaspoon of chili powder.
4. Drizzle 1 tablespoon of lime juice over the mixture, toss gently, and cook for an additional 2 minutes until heated through.
5. Season with salt and pepper as desired and serve immediately.

Nutritional Info (per serving): kcal 330 | pro 28g | carbs 10g | fat 15g

---

Express Eggplant Parmesan Bake

Servings: 1 person

Prep Time: 30 minutes

Ingredients:
- 1 small eggplant (sliced into 1/4-inch rounds)
- 1/2 cup low-fat marinara sauce (no added sugar)
- 1/4 cup shredded low-fat mozzarella cheese
- 1 tablespoon grated Parmesan cheese
- Salt, to taste
- Pepper, to taste

Possible Variations:
For extra flavor, consider sprinkling Italian herbs such as oregano or basil over the top before baking, or substitute the mozzarella with low-fat provolone for a slightly different taste.

Preparation:
1. Preheat your oven to 375°F.
2. Arrange the eggplant slices on a lightly greased baking sheet and season them with salt and pepper.
3. Spoon 1/2 cup of low-fat marinara sauce evenly over the eggplant slices, then top each slice with shredded mozzarella and a sprinkle of grated Parmesan.
4. Bake in the preheated oven for 20 minutes until the eggplant is tender and the cheese is melted and lightly golden.
5. Remove from the oven and serve warm immediately.

Nutritional Info (per serving): kcal 340 | pro 22g | carbs 12g | fat 16g

Wholesome Tofu & Spinach Stir-Fry

Servings: 1 bowl | **Prep Time:** 25 minutes

Ingredients:
- 4 oz firm tofu (cubed)
- 1 cup fresh spinach
- 1/2 cup sliced red bell pepper
- 1 tablespoon low-sodium soy sauce
- 1 teaspoon olive oil
- Salt, to taste

Possible Variations:
For a firmer texture, you can substitute tofu with tempeh. Adding a dash of chili flakes can give the dish an extra spicy kick, or you might swap red bell pepper with yellow bell pepper for a sweeter note.

Preparation:
1. Heat 1 teaspoon of olive oil in a non-stick skillet over medium heat.
2. Add the cubed tofu and sauté for about 4–5 minutes until the tofu is lightly golden.
3. Add the sliced red bell pepper and fresh spinach to the skillet and stir-fry for another 3–4 minutes until the spinach wilts and the bell pepper softens.
4. Drizzle with 1 tablespoon low-sodium soy sauce, season with salt, toss gently, and serve immediately.

Nutritional Info (per serving): kcal 320 | pro 20g | carbs 10g | fat 18g

---

Lightning Beef Zoodle Bowl

Servings: 1 bowl | **Prep Time:** 25 minutes

Ingredients:
- 4 oz lean beef strips (pre-cooked)
- 1 medium zucchini (spiralized into noodles)
- 1/2 cup halved cherry tomatoes
- 1 tablespoon olive oil
- Salt, to taste
- Pepper, to taste

Possible Variations:
For a brighter flavor, you can add a squeeze of lemon juice or substitute the beef with grilled chicken for a lighter option.

Preparation:
1. Heat 1 tablespoon of olive oil in a non-stick skillet over medium heat.
2. Add the spiralized zucchini noodles and halved cherry tomatoes to the skillet and sauté for 3–4 minutes until the zucchini is tender.
3. Stir in the pre-cooked lean beef strips and toss gently to combine all ingredients.
4. Season with salt and pepper to taste, then serve immediately.

Nutritional Info (per serving): kcal 340 | pro 28g | carbs 8g | fat 16g

STRESS-FREE SNACKS

Bite-Sized Boosts for Any Time

Snacking can be a lifesaver during busy days, but it doesn't have to derail your high-protein, low-carb lifestyle. In this category, you'll find a collection of simple, delicious snack recipes that are designed to keep hunger at bay without sacrificing nutrition.

These stress-free snacks are perfect for work breaks, on-the-go moments, or whenever you need a quick boost of energy. Enjoy these bite-sized treats that make healthy eating effortless and satisfying—so you can stay fueled and focused all day long.

Crunchy Almond Energy Bites

Servings: 1 person

Prep Time: 15 minutes (plus 20 minutes chilling)

Ingredients:
- 1/2 cup almond butter
- 1/4 cup vanilla protein powder
- 1/4 cup chopped almonds
- 2 tablespoons chia seeds
- 1 teaspoon honey (optional)
- 1/4 cup unsweetened shredded coconut

Possible Variations:
You can substitute chopped almonds with walnuts or pecans, or omit the honey and use a few drops of stevia for a sugar-free option.

Preparation:
1. In a bowl, whisk together almond butter, vanilla protein powder, chia seeds, and honey until you have a smooth mixture.
2. Carefully fold in the chopped almonds and unsweetened shredded coconut until evenly distributed.
3. Roll the mixture into small bite-sized balls and place them on a parchment-lined tray.
4. Refrigerate for at least 20 minutes until firm, then enjoy your energy bites as a quick, nutritious snack.

Nutritional Info (per serving): kcal 150 | pro 8g | carbs 6g | fat 10g

Zesty Tuna Cucumber Cups

Servings: 1 person (yield: 2 cucumber cups)

Prep Time: 10 minutes

Ingredients:
- 1 can tuna in water (drained)
- 1 tablespoon plain Greek yogurt
- 1 teaspoon lemon juice
- Salt, to taste
- Pepper, to taste
- 1/2 cucumber (cut into thick rounds)

Possible Variations:
You can enhance the flavor by adding diced celery or capers to the tuna mixture, or substitute the Greek yogurt with mashed avocado for a creamier texture.

Preparation:
1. In a bowl, mix together all the ingredients by combining the drained tuna, plain Greek yogurt, lemon juice, salt, and pepper until well blended.
2. Spoon the mixture evenly into the thick cucumber rounds to form two easy-to-eat cups.
3. Serve immediately as a refreshing, protein-packed snack.

Nutritional Info (per serving): kcal 280 | pro 25g | carbs 5g | fat 18g

Spicy Turkey Jerky Bites

Servings: 1 person

Prep Time: 20 minutes

Ingredients:
- 4 oz lean turkey breast (pre-cooked, thinly sliced)
- 1/2 teaspoon chili powder
- 1/4 teaspoon garlic powder
- 1 teaspoon olive oil
- 1 teaspoon lime juice
- Salt, to taste

Possible Variations:
For a milder flavor, reduce the chili powder or omit it entirely, and add a splash more lime juice for extra tang.

Preparation:
1. In a bowl, toss the pre-cooked turkey slices with chili powder, garlic powder, olive oil, lime juice, and salt until evenly coated.
2. Heat a non-stick skillet over medium-high heat and add the seasoned turkey slices.
3. Sear the turkey slices for about 3–4 minutes on each side until they are crisp around the edges.
4. Remove from the skillet and serve immediately as a spicy, protein-rich snack.

Nutritional Info (per serving): kcal 310 | pro 28g | carbs 7g | fat 15g

---

Savory Veggie Hummus Cups

Servings: 1 person (yield: 2 cups)

Prep Time: 10 minutes

Ingredients:
- 2 mini bell peppers (halved and seeded)
- 1/4 cup hummus
- 1/4 cup diced cucumber
- Salt, to taste
- Pepper, to taste

Possible Variations:
You might drizzle a little olive oil over the hummus or sprinkle a pinch of paprika for an extra flavor boost. Alternatively, you could mix finely diced tomatoes into the hummus before filling the peppers.

Preparation:
1. Halve the mini bell peppers lengthwise and remove the seeds.
2. Fill each bell pepper half by spooning the hummus into it, then top with the diced cucumber.
3. Season lightly with salt and pepper, and serve immediately as a portable, savory snack.

Nutritional Info (per serving): kcal 150 | pro 6g | carbs 10g | fat 8g

Cheddar Cauliflower Popper Bites

Servings: 1 bowl (yield: about 8 bite-sized pieces) **Prep Time:** 25 minutes

Ingredients:
- 1 cup cauliflower florets (cut into bite-sized pieces)
- 1/4 cup shredded low-fat cheddar cheese
- 1 large egg (beaten)
- Salt, to taste
- Pepper, to taste
- 1 teaspoon olive oil

Possible Variations:
For an extra kick, add a pinch of garlic powder or paprika before baking, or substitute the cheddar cheese with crumbled feta for a tangier flavor.

Preparation:
1. Preheat your oven to 400°F.
2. In a bowl, combine the cauliflower florets with the beaten egg, shredded cheddar cheese, olive oil, salt, and pepper until the florets are evenly coated.
3. Spread the mixture on a parchment-lined baking sheet in a single layer.
4. Bake for 15 minutes until the cauliflower is tender and the cheese is melted and lightly browned.
5. Remove from the oven and serve immediately as crunchy, cheesy popper bites.

Nutritional Info (per serving): kcal 180 | pro 12g | carbs 8g | fat 10g

Nutty Seed Crunch Clusters

Servings: 1 person **Prep Time:** 15 minutes (plus 20 minutes chilling)

Ingredients:
- 1/2 cup almond butter
- 1/4 cup vanilla protein powder
- 2 tablespoons chia seeds
- 2 tablespoons pumpkin seeds
- 2 tablespoons unsweetened shredded coconut
- 1 teaspoon honey (optional)

Possible Variations:
You can experiment by swapping pumpkin seeds with sunflower seeds or using a few drops of stevia instead of honey for a sugar-free option. Enjoy these clusters as a crunchy, portable snack to boost your day!

Preparation:
1. In a bowl, combine the almond butter, vanilla protein powder, and chia seeds until the mixture is smooth.
2. Gently fold in the pumpkin seeds and unsweetened shredded coconut.
3. If desired, stir in the honey for a touch of sweetness.
4. Roll the mixture into small clusters and arrange them on a parchment-lined tray.
5. Refrigerate for at least 20 minutes until firm, then enjoy your nutty seed crunch clusters as a quick, energizing snack.

Nutritional Info (per serving): kcal 150 | pro 8g | carbs 6g | fat 10g

Avocado Lime Crisps

Servings: 1 person

Prep Time: 15 minutes

Ingredients:
- 1 ripe avocado
- 1 tablespoon lime juice
- 1 teaspoon olive oil
- Salt, to taste
- 1/4 teaspoon cayenne pepper (optional)

Possible Variations:
For a different twist, you might substitute lime juice with lemon juice or sprinkle lime zest over the crisps after baking for an extra burst of flavor.

Preparation:
1. Preheat your oven to 375°F.
2. Thinly slice the avocado and toss the slices with lime juice, olive oil, salt, and cayenne pepper if you're using it.
3. Arrange the avocado slices in a single layer on a parchment-lined baking sheet.
4. Bake for 10–12 minutes until the edges are crisp.
5. Allow to cool slightly and enjoy these zesty crisps as a refreshing snack.

Nutritional Info (per serving): kcal 200 | pro 3g | carbs 10g | fat 16g

Protein-Packed Cottage Cheese Medallions

Servings: 1 person (yield: 4 medallions)

Prep Time: 15 minutes

Ingredients:
- 1 cup low-fat cottage cheese
- 1/4 cup almond flour
- 1 egg white
- Salt, to taste
- Pepper, to taste
- 1 teaspoon olive oil

Possible Variations:
You can swap almond flour with coconut flour for a different texture, or add a pinch of dried herbs into the mixture for an extra flavor boost.

Preparation:
1. In a bowl, combine the low-fat cottage cheese, almond flour, egg white, salt, and pepper until the mixture is smooth.
2. Form the mixture into 4 small medallions.
3. Heat the olive oil in a non-stick skillet over medium heat.
4. Cook the medallions for 3–4 minutes on each side until they turn golden and firm.
5. Serve warm as a satisfying, protein-rich snack.

Nutritional Info (per serving): kcal 250 | pro 25g | carbs 10g | fat 8g

Smokin' Paprika Beef Jerky

Servings: 1 person

Prep Time: 20 minutes

Ingredients:
- 4 oz lean beef strips (pre-cooked, thinly sliced)
- 1/2 teaspoon smoked paprika
- 1/4 teaspoon garlic powder
- 1 teaspoon olive oil
- Salt, to taste

Possible Variations:
For a milder version, you may reduce the smoked paprika or omit it altogether and add a splash of lime juice for extra tang.

Preparation:
1. In a bowl, toss the pre-cooked beef strips with smoked paprika, garlic powder, olive oil, and salt until they are evenly coated.
2. Heat a non-stick skillet over medium-high heat and add the seasoned beef strips.
3. Sear for 3–4 minutes on each side until the edges become crisp.
4. Remove from the skillet and serve immediately as a savory, spicy snack.

Nutritional Info (per serving): kcal 310 | pro 28g | carbs 7g | fat 15g

---

Mini Egg Salad Lettuce Wraps

Servings: 1 person (yield: 2 wraps)

Prep Time: 15 minutes

Ingredients:
- 3 hard-boiled eggs, chopped
- 1 tablespoon plain Greek yogurt
- 1 teaspoon Dijon mustard
- Salt, to taste
- Pepper, to taste
- 2 large butter lettuce leaves

Possible Variations:
You might add finely chopped celery for extra crunch or a dash of hot sauce for a spicy twist, enhancing the flavor while keeping the snack light and nutritious.

Preparation:
1. In a bowl, combine the chopped hard-boiled eggs, plain Greek yogurt, and Dijon mustard, mixing until the egg salad is smooth; season with salt and pepper.
2. Spoon the egg salad evenly into 2 large butter lettuce leaves, forming two convenient wraps.
3. Serve immediately as a light, portable snack.

Nutritional Info (per serving): kcal 280 | pro 18g | carbs 5g | fat 20g

Quinoa Veggie Protein Balls

Servings: 1 person (yield: about 8 balls) **Prep Time:** 15 minutes (plus 15 minutes chilling)

Ingredients:
- 1/2 cup cooked quinoa (pre-cooked)
- 1/4 cup grated zucchini (squeezed of excess water)
- 1 large egg (lightly beaten)
- 2 tablespoons almond flour
- Salt and pepper, to taste

Possible Variations:
You can enhance the nutty flavor by adding a tablespoon of chopped walnuts, or substitute almond flour with coconut flour for a different texture.

Preparation:
1. In a bowl, mix all the ingredients until a uniform mixture forms.
2. Roll the mixture into small, bite-sized balls and arrange them on a parchment-lined tray.
3. Refrigerate for at least 15 minutes until firm, then serve as a protein-packed, portable snack.

Nutritional Info (per serving): kcal 210 | pro 12g | carbs 18g | fat 8g

---

Chicken Caesar Snack Cups

Servings: 1 person (yield: 2 lettuce cups) **Prep Time:** 15 minutes

Ingredients:
- 3 oz grilled chicken breast (pre-cooked, chopped)
- 1 tablespoon light Caesar dressing
- 1 tablespoon grated Parmesan cheese
- Salt and pepper, to taste
- 2 large romaine lettuce leaves

Possible Variations:
If you like, add a squeeze of lemon juice or a few capers to boost the tang, or swap Caesar dressing with a light Greek yogurt-based dressing for a creamier texture.

Preparation:
1. In a bowl, mix together the pre-cooked chicken, light Caesar dressing, and grated Parmesan cheese until well blended.
2. Spoon the chicken Caesar mixture evenly into 2 large romaine lettuce leaves, forming crisp and convenient snack cups.
3. Serve immediately for a quick, savory bite that's perfect on the go.

Nutritional Info (per serving): kcal 300 | pro 25g | carbs 5g | fat 15g

Tangy Mediterranean Olive Bites

Servings: 1 person (yield: about 10 bites) **Prep Time:** 10 minutes

Ingredients:
- 10 large pitted Kalamata olives
- 2 oz crumbled low-fat feta cheese
- 1 teaspoon lemon juice
- 1/4 teaspoon dried oregano
- A drizzle of extra virgin olive oil
- Salt, to taste

Possible Variations:
You can use green olives instead of Kalamata or add a small dash of crushed red pepper flakes into the feta mixture for a subtle kick.

Preparation:
1. In a bowl, mix all the ingredients by combining the crumbled feta with lemon juice, dried oregano, a drizzle of extra virgin olive oil, and a pinch of salt until the mixture is smooth.
2. Carefully stuff each pitted Kalamata olive with a small amount of the feta mixture.
3. Arrange the stuffed olives on a plate and serve immediately as a tangy, bite-sized treat.

Nutritional Info (per serving): kcal 150 | pro 4g | carbs 3g | fat 12g

Kale & Parmesan Crisps

Servings: 1 person **Prep Time:** 15 minutes

Ingredients:
- 1 cup kale leaves (stems removed, torn into bite-sized pieces)
- 1 tablespoon olive oil
- 1/4 cup shredded low-fat Parmesan cheese
- Salt and pepper, to taste
- (Optional: 1/4 teaspoon garlic powder)

Possible Variations:
You might substitute kale with baby spinach or arugula for a different green crunch, or add a squeeze of lemon juice after baking for an extra burst of freshness.

Preparation:
1. Preheat your oven to 350°F.
2. In a bowl, toss the kale with olive oil, salt, pepper, and garlic powder (if using) until the leaves are evenly coated.
3. Spread the kale in a single layer on a parchment-lined baking sheet and sprinkle the shredded Parmesan cheese over the top.
4. Bake for 10–12 minutes until the kale is crispy and the cheese is lightly golden.
5. Remove from the oven, let cool slightly, and serve immediately as crunchy, flavorful crisps.

Nutritional Info (per serving): kcal 180 | pro 8g | carbs 6g | fat 10g

Tofu Satay Protein Nuggets

Servings: 1 person

Prep Time: 20 minutes

Ingredients:
- 4 oz firm tofu (cubed)
- 1 tablespoon natural peanut butter
- 1 teaspoon low-sodium soy sauce
- 1/2 teaspoon curry powder
- Salt, to taste
- 1 teaspoon olive oil

Possible Variations:
For a different flavor profile, try substituting natural peanut butter with almond butter, or adjust the curry powder level to suit your spice preference. You could also swap tofu with tempeh for a firmer texture.

Preparation:
1. In a bowl, mix together all the ingredients by gently tossing the tofu cubes with natural peanut butter, low-sodium soy sauce, curry powder, olive oil, and a pinch of salt until each piece is evenly coated.
2. Heat a non-stick skillet over medium heat and add the seasoned tofu cubes.
3. Sauté for about 6–7 minutes, turning occasionally, until the tofu is heated through and slightly crispy on all sides.
4. Serve immediately as a protein-packed, flavorful snack.

Nutritional Info (per serving): kcal 320 | pro 20g | carbs 10g | fat 18g

---

Spicy Shrimp Cocktail Cups

Servings: 1 person (yield: 2 cups)

Prep Time: 10 minutes

Ingredients:
- 4 oz pre-cooked shrimp
- 1/2 small cucumber (cut into thick rounds)
- 1 teaspoon lime juice
- 1/4 teaspoon chili powder
- Salt, to taste

Possible Variations:
For an extra burst of flavor, consider adding finely diced celery or capers to the shrimp mixture, or swap Greek yogurt for a creamier texture if desired.

Preparation:
1. Slice the cucumber into 2 thick rounds to serve as cups.
2. In a bowl, combine the pre-cooked shrimp with lime juice, chili powder, and salt until evenly coated.
3. Spoon the shrimp mixture evenly into each cucumber round.
4. Serve immediately as a refreshing, protein-packed snack.

Nutritional Info (per serving): kcal 280 | pro 25g | carbs 5g | fat 18g

Zoodle Veggie Crunch Bites

Servings: 1 person (yield: about 6 bites)

Prep Time: 20 minutes

Ingredients:
- 1 medium zucchini (spiralized into noodles)
- 1/4 cup grated carrot
- 1 tablespoon almond flour
- 1 egg white
- Salt, to taste
- Pepper, to taste

Possible Variations:
For a nuttier flavor, add a tablespoon of chopped walnuts to the mixture, or substitute almond flour with coconut flour for a slightly different texture.

Preparation:
1. In a bowl, combine the spiralized zucchini, grated carrot, almond flour, egg white, salt, and pepper until a uniform mixture forms.
2. Form the mixture into small bite-sized patties.
3. Heat a non-stick skillet over medium heat and add a light coating of cooking spray.
4. Cook the patties for about 3–4 minutes per side until they are lightly crisp on the outside.
5. Remove from the skillet and serve immediately as crunchy, veggie-packed bites.

Nutritional Info (per serving): kcal 210 | pro 12g | carbs 18g | fat 8g

Greek Yogurt Berry Burst Cups

Servings: 1 person (yield: 2 cups)

Prep Time: 5 minutes

Ingredients:
- 1 cup plain Greek yogurt
- 1/2 cup mixed fresh berries
- 1 tablespoon chopped walnuts
- 1 teaspoon honey (optional)
- A pinch of cinnamon

Possible Variations:
You can substitute walnuts with pecans or almonds, or experiment by adding a few drops of vanilla extract to enhance the flavor.

Preparation:
1. Spoon the plain Greek yogurt evenly into 2 small serving cups.
2. Top each cup with mixed fresh berries and a sprinkle of chopped walnuts.
3. Drizzle with honey (if using) and finish with a light dusting of cinnamon.
4. Serve immediately as a delicious, energizing snack.

Nutritional Info (per serving): kcal 240 | pro 15g | carbs 14g | fat 10g

Power Chia Pudding Poppers

Servings: 1 person (yield: about 8 poppers)

Prep Time: 5 minutes (plus overnight chilling)

Ingredients:
- 1 cup unsweetened almond milk
- 3 tablespoons chia seeds
- 1 scoop vanilla protein powder
- 1/2 teaspoon vanilla extract
- A few fresh berries for topping

Possible Variations:
You may substitute unsweetened almond milk with coconut milk for a different flavor, or add a pinch of cinnamon to the mixture before chilling.

Preparation:
1. In a jar, combine unsweetened almond milk, chia seeds, vanilla protein powder, and vanilla extract; stir until the mixture is smooth.
2. Cover and refrigerate overnight (or for at least 4 hours) until the mixture thickens into a pudding-like consistency.
3. In the morning, stir the pudding and use a small spoon or melon baller to scoop out bite-sized portions, then top each popper with a fresh berry.
4. Serve chilled as a refreshing, protein-rich snack.

Nutritional Info (per serving): kcal 250 | pro 20g | carbs 12g | fat 12g

Turbo Nutty Trail Mix

Servings: 1 person

Prep Time: 5 minutes

Ingredients:
- 1/4 cup chopped almonds
- 1/4 cup chopped walnuts
- 1/4 cup pumpkin seeds
- 1/4 cup unsweetened dried cranberries
- 1 tablespoon unsweetened coconut flakes
- A pinch of cinnamon

Possible Variations:
Feel free to experiment by substituting walnuts with pecans or adding a few dried blueberries for extra tang, making sure to adjust the quantities to maintain a balanced mix.

Preparation:
1. In a bowl, combine chopped almonds, walnuts, pumpkin seeds, unsweetened dried cranberries, coconut flakes, and a pinch of cinnamon.
2. Toss the ingredients together until well mixed.
3. Serve immediately as a quick, energizing trail mix snack.

Nutritional Info (per serving): kcal 300 | pro 10g | carbs 15g | fat 20g

LIGHT DESSERTS

Sweet Treats Without the Guilt

Indulging in dessert doesn't have to mean sacrificing your healthy lifestyle. In this category, you'll discover a range of light desserts that satisfy your sweet cravings while keeping with your high-protein, low-carb goals.

These recipes are designed to be both delicious and nutritious, proving that you can enjoy a sweet finish to your meal without derailing your progress.

Perfect for a family treat or a special solo moment of indulgence, these desserts let you enjoy the best of both worlds—sweet satisfaction and mindful eating. Enjoy exploring these guilt-free delights that prove healthy eating can be fun and flavorful!

Velvety Dark Chocolate Avocado Mousse

Servings: 1 person

Prep Time: 10 minutes (plus 30 minutes chilling)

Ingredients:
- 1 ripe avocado
- 1 tablespoon unsweetened cocoa powder
- 1 teaspoon honey (or stevia, optional)
- 1/2 teaspoon vanilla extract
- Pinch of salt

Possible Variations:
For an extra touch of brightness, top with a few fresh raspberries or a sprinkle of cocoa nibs. You can also adjust the sweetness by experimenting with different natural sweeteners.

Preparation:
1. Place all the ingredients into a blender and blend until the mixture is completely smooth.
2. Transfer the mousse into a serving bowl.
3. Refrigerate for at least 30 minutes until well chilled and thickened.
4. Serve immediately for a rich, velvety dessert.

Nutritional Info (per serving): kcal 220 | pro 4g | carbs 15g | fat 16g

---

Tropical Coconut Berry Bliss Parfait

Servings: 1 person

Prep Time: 5 minutes

Ingredients:
- 1 cup unsweetened coconut yogurt
- 1/2 cup mixed fresh berries (blueberries, strawberries, raspberries)
- 2 tablespoons toasted coconut flakes
- 1 teaspoon honey (optional)

Possible Variations:
If you prefer a tangier taste, substitute the coconut yogurt with plain Greek yogurt, or add a few kiwi slices for an extra tropical twist.

Preparation:
1. In a serving glass, layer the unsweetened coconut yogurt and mixed fresh berries.
2. Drizzle with honey if desired, then top with toasted coconut flakes.
3. Enjoy immediately for a refreshing, tropical burst of flavor.

Nutritional Info (per serving): kcal 240 | pro 8g | carbs 18g | fat 14g

Luscious Vanilla Protein Pudding Delight

Servings: 1 person

Prep Time: 5 minutes (plus overnight chilling)

Ingredients:
- 1 cup unsweetened almond milk
- 1 scoop vanilla protein powder
- 3 tablespoons chia seeds
- 1/2 teaspoon vanilla extract
- Sweetener of choice (optional)

Possible Variations:
You may top the pudding with a few fresh berries or a sprinkle of cinnamon for added warmth. Coconut milk can also be used instead of almond milk for a creamier flavor.

Preparation:
1. In a jar, combine the unsweetened almond milk, vanilla protein powder, chia seeds, vanilla extract, and your chosen sweetener if desired; stir until smooth.
2. Cover and refrigerate overnight (or for at least 4 hours) until the mixture thickens to a pudding-like consistency.
3. Stir well before serving and enjoy your protein-rich pudding.

Nutritional Info (per serving): kcal 250 | pro 20g | carbs 12g | fat 12g

---

Cinnamon-Spiced Apple Crisp Fantasy

Servings: 1 person

Prep Time: 30 minutes

Ingredients:
- 1 medium apple, cored and diced
- 2 tablespoons almond flour
- 1 tablespoon rolled oats
- 1/2 teaspoon ground cinnamon
- 1 teaspoon coconut oil
- Sweetener of choice (optional)

Possible Variations:
For a lower-carb version, substitute the rolled oats with additional almond flour. You can also add a few chopped nuts for extra crunch or a dash of nutmeg for added spice.

Preparation:
1. Preheat your oven to 375°F.
2. In a bowl, combine the diced apple with almond flour, rolled oats, ground cinnamon, coconut oil, and sweetener if desired; mix until the apple is evenly coated.
3. Spread the mixture evenly in a small baking dish.
4. Bake for 20–25 minutes until the apple is tender and the topping is golden brown.
5. Serve warm for a comforting, sweet treat.

Nutritional Info (per serving): kcal 260 | pro 4g | carbs 28g | fat 12g

Zesty Lemon Chia Radiance

Servings: 1 person

Prep Time: 5 minutes (plus overnight chilling)

Ingredients:
- 1 cup unsweetened almond milk
- 3 tablespoons chia seeds
- 1 scoop vanilla protein powder (optional)
- 1 tablespoon lemon juice
- Zest of 1/2 lemon
- Sweetener of choice (optional)

Possible Variations:
For a richer taste, substitute almond milk with coconut milk, or add a few blueberries on top before serving for an extra burst of flavor.

Preparation:
1. Combine all the ingredients in a jar—unsweetened almond milk, chia seeds, vanilla protein powder (if using), lemon juice, lemon zest, and sweetener if desired—and stir until completely smooth.
2. Cover the jar and refrigerate overnight (or for at least 4 hours) until the mixture thickens to a pudding-like consistency.
3. Stir well before serving, and enjoy this refreshing, tangy dessert.

Nutritional Info (per serving): kcal 240 | pro 20g | carbs 12g | fat 12g

---

Berry Burst Frozen Yogurt Jewels

Servings: 1 person (yield: about 8 jewels)

Prep Time: 10 minutes (plus 30 minutes freezing)

Ingredients:
- 1 cup plain Greek yogurt
- 1/2 cup mixed fresh berries (blueberries, strawberries, raspberries)
- 1 teaspoon vanilla extract
- 1 teaspoon honey (optional)
- 1/4 cup finely chopped almonds

Possible Variations:
You can swap the almonds with chopped walnuts or pecans for a different nutty flavor, or add a few mint leaves into the blender for a cool twist.

Preparation:
1. Combine all the ingredients—Greek yogurt, mixed berries, vanilla extract, and honey (if using)—in a blender and blend until smooth.
2. Pour the mixture into an ice cube tray or silicone mold, and sprinkle the finely chopped almonds evenly on top of each portion.
3. Freeze for at least 30 minutes until set, then pop out the jewels and serve immediately for a refreshing, high-protein frozen treat.

Nutritional Info (per serving): kcal 220 | pro 18g | carbs 15g | fat 10g

Minty Matcha Coconut Dream Bars

Servings: 1 person (yield: 4 bars)

Prep Time: 25 minutes (plus 30 minutes chilling)

Ingredients:
- 1/2 cup unsweetened shredded coconut
- 2 tablespoons coconut flour
- 1 tablespoon almond butter
- 1 egg white
- 1/2 teaspoon matcha powder
- Sweetener of choice (optional)

Possible Variations:
You may experiment by adding a few drops of peppermint extract for an extra minty flavor or substituting almond butter with cashew butter.

Preparation:
1. Preheat your oven to 350°F.
2. In a bowl, whisk together all the ingredients—unsweetened shredded coconut, coconut flour, almond butter, egg white, matcha powder, and sweetener (if using)—until the batter is smooth.
3. Press the mixture evenly into a small, parchment-lined baking pan, forming a compact layer.
4. Bake for 15 minutes until the edges are lightly golden.
5. Remove from the oven, let cool, then cut into 4 bars and serve as a refreshing, high-protein snack.

Nutritional Info (per serving): kcal 240 | pro 12g | carbs 12g | fat 14g

Guiltless Almond Butter Fudge Indulgence

Servings: 1 person (yield: 6 fudge squares)

Prep Time: 20 minutes (plus 20 minutes chilling)

Ingredients:
- 1/2 cup natural almond butter
- 1 scoop chocolate protein powder
- 1 tablespoon unsweetened cocoa powder
- 1 tablespoon coconut oil
- 1-2 teaspoons unsweetened almond milk (adjust as needed)
- Sweetener of choice (optional)

Possible Variations:
You can swap almond butter with cashew butter for a different nutty flavor, or add a pinch of cinnamon for extra warmth.

Preparation:
1. In a microwave-safe bowl, gently heat the almond butter and coconut oil until melted and easily stirrable.
2. Stir in the chocolate protein powder, unsweetened cocoa powder, and sweetener (if using) until the mixture is smooth.
3. Add unsweetened almond milk gradually to achieve a thick, fudgy consistency.
4. Pour the mixture into a small, parchment-lined tray and spread it evenly.
5. Refrigerate for at least 20 minutes until the fudge is firm, then cut into 6 squares and serve.

Nutritional Info (per serving): kcal 300 | pro 20g | carbs 10g | fat 18g

Fluffy Protein Pancake Sundae Surprise

Servings: 1 person (yields 3 small pancakes)

Prep Time: 20 minutes

Ingredients:
- 1/2 cup almond flour
- 1 large egg
- 1/4 cup unsweetened almond milk
- 1/2 teaspoon vanilla extract
- Toppings: 1/2 cup plain Greek yogurt, 1/4 cup mixed fresh berries

Possible Variations:
Feel free to swap mixed berries with sliced bananas (adjusting carb count) or add a drizzle of sugar-free syrup for extra indulgence.

Preparation:
1. In a bowl, mix together almond flour, egg, unsweetened almond milk, and vanilla extract until a smooth pancake batter forms.
2. Heat a non-stick skillet over medium heat and lightly coat with cooking spray.
3. Spoon small rounds of the batter onto the skillet and cook for 2–3 minutes on each side until golden and set.
4. Stack the 3 pancakes on a plate, top with plain Greek yogurt and fresh berries, and serve immediately as a fun, high-protein sundae-like breakfast.

Nutritional Info (per serving): kcal 300 | pro 15g | carbs 10g | fat 22g

---

Decadent Cocoa Protein Fudge Bliss

Servings: 1 person (yield: 6 fudge squares)

Prep Time: 20 minutes (plus 20 minutes chilling)

Ingredients:
- 1/2 cup almond butter
- 1 scoop chocolate protein powder
- 2 tablespoons unsweetened cocoa powder
- 1 tablespoon coconut oil
- 1-2 teaspoons unsweetened almond milk (adjust as needed)
- Sweetener of choice (optional)

Possible Variations:
For a different twist, substitute coconut oil with a bit of melted dark chocolate or try adding a pinch of espresso powder to enhance the cocoa flavor.

Preparation:
1. In a bowl, combine almond butter, chocolate protein powder, and unsweetened cocoa powder.
2. Gently mix in coconut oil and unsweetened almond milk until a smooth, thick fudge mixture forms; add sweetener if desired.
3. Spread the mixture evenly into a small, parchment-lined tray.
4. Refrigerate for at least 20 minutes until set, then cut into 6 squares and serve as a rich, satisfying dessert.

Nutritional Info (per serving): kcal 320 | pro 20g | carbs 12g | fat 18g

Peach Perfection Protein Custard

Servings: 1 person

Prep Time: 25 minutes

Ingredients:
- 1 ripe peach, peeled and diced
- 1/2 cup unsweetened almond milk
- 1 scoop vanilla protein powder
- 1 large egg white
- A pinch of cinnamon
- Sweetener of choice (optional)

Possible Variations:
You can substitute the peach with a nectarine for a different flavor profile, or add a dash of nutmeg along with the cinnamon for extra spice.

Preparation:
1. Preheat your oven to 350°F.
2. In a bowl, combine all the ingredients—diced peach, unsweetened almond milk, vanilla protein powder, egg white, a pinch of cinnamon, and sweetener (if using)—until the mixture is smooth.
3. Pour the mixture into a small ramekin or baking dish.
4. Bake for 20–25 minutes until the custard is set and slightly puffed.
5. Remove from the oven, let cool slightly, and serve warm or chilled.

Nutritional Info (per serving): kcal 240 | pro 20g | carbs 18g | fat 8g

Refreshing Raspberry Lime Sorbet

Servings: 1 person

Prep Time: 10 minutes (plus freezing time)

Ingredients:
- 1 cup frozen raspberries
- 1 tablespoon lime juice
- 1/2 cup water
- Sweetener of choice (optional)
- A pinch of salt

Possible Variations:
For a creamier texture, you can substitute water with unsweetened almond milk or add a few mint leaves during blending for a cool twist.

Preparation:
1. Place all the ingredients into a blender and blend until the mixture is smooth.
2. Pour the blend into a shallow container and freeze for 30 minutes to 1 hour, stirring occasionally until a smooth sorbet consistency is achieved.
3. Serve immediately for a refreshing, tangy dessert.

Nutritional Info (per serving): kcal 180 | pro 2g | carbs 20g | fat 2g

Wholesome Pumpkin Spice Velvet Pudding

Servings: 1 person **Prep Time:** 5 minutes (plus overnight chilling)

Ingredients:
- 1/2 cup unsweetened pumpkin puree
- 1/2 cup unsweetened almond milk
- 1 scoop vanilla protein powder
- 1/2 teaspoon pumpkin pie spice
- Sweetener of choice (optional)
- A pinch of salt

Possible Variations:
You may add a splash of vanilla extract for extra depth or top with a few crushed walnuts for added texture.

Preparation:
1. In a bowl, combine all the ingredients—unsweetened pumpkin puree, unsweetened almond milk, vanilla protein powder, pumpkin pie spice, sweetener (if using), and a pinch of salt—until the mixture is smooth.
2. Pour the mixture into a serving jar or bowl, cover, and refrigerate overnight (or for at least 4 hours) until the pudding thickens to a velvety consistency.
3. Stir well before serving and enjoy this seasonal, nutritious treat chilled or at room temperature.

Nutritional Info (per serving): kcal 220 | pro 20g | carbs 15g | fat 8g

Crispy Baked Cinnamon-Kissed Pears

Servings: 1 person **Prep Time:** 20 minutes

Ingredients:
- 1 medium pear, thinly sliced
- 2 teaspoons almond flour
- 1 teaspoon coconut oil
- 1 teaspoon ground cinnamon
- Sweetener of choice (optional)
- A pinch of salt

Possible Variations:
For a lower-carb option, reduce the amount of sweetener or substitute with a touch of almond butter; you may also add chopped nuts for extra crunch or a dash of nutmeg for additional spice.

Preparation:
1. Preheat your oven to 375°F.
2. In a bowl, toss the thinly sliced pear with almond flour, coconut oil, ground cinnamon, a pinch of salt, and sweetener if desired until evenly coated.
3. Arrange the pear slices in a single layer on a parchment-lined baking sheet.
4. Bake for 15–20 minutes until the edges are crisp and the slices are tender.
5. Remove from the oven, allow to cool slightly, and serve as a warm, comforting dessert.

Nutritional Info (per serving): kcal 240 | pro 4g | carbs 28g | fat 12g

Vanilla Chia & Mixed Berry Symphony

Servings: 1 person

Prep Time: 5 minutes (plus overnight chilling)

Ingredients:
- 1 cup unsweetened almond milk
- 3 tablespoons chia seeds
- 1 scoop vanilla protein powder
- 1/2 teaspoon vanilla extract
- 1/2 cup mixed fresh berries
- Sweetener of choice (optional)

Possible Variations:
For a creamier texture, you may substitute almond milk with coconut milk, or drizzle a little honey on top if extra sweetness is desired.

Preparation:
1. In a bowl or jar, combine unsweetened almond milk, chia seeds, vanilla protein powder, and vanilla extract; stir until the mixture is smooth.
2. Cover and refrigerate overnight (or for at least 4 hours) until the mixture thickens to a pudding-like consistency.
3. Gently fold in the mixed fresh berries before serving.
4. Enjoy chilled as a vibrant, nutritious dessert.

Nutritional Info (per serving): kcal 240 | pro 20g | carbs 12g | fat 12g

---

Choco-Banana Protein Ice Cream Delight

Servings: 1 person

Prep Time: 5 minutes (plus 10 minutes freezing)

Ingredients:
- 1 frozen banana
- 1 scoop chocolate protein powder
- 1/4 cup unsweetened almond milk
- 1 teaspoon unsweetened cocoa powder
- 1/2 teaspoon vanilla extract

Possible Variations:
For a lower-carb option, replace half of the banana with frozen avocado to reduce sugars while maintaining a creamy texture. You can also top it with crushed nuts or sugar-free chocolate chips for added crunch.

Preparation:
1. Blend all the ingredients until smooth and creamy.
2. Pour the mixture into a container and freeze for about 10 minutes until it firms up slightly.
3. Serve immediately for a soft-serve consistency or freeze for an additional 5–10 minutes for a firmer texture.

Nutritional Info (per serving): kcal 220 | pro 22g | carbs 24g | fat 4g

No-Bake Peanut Butter Protein Bliss Bars

Servings: 6 bars

Prep Time: 10 minutes (plus 30 minutes chilling)

Ingredients:
- 1/2 cup natural peanut butter (no added sugar)
- 1 scoop vanilla protein powder
- 2 tablespoons almond flour
- 1 tablespoon unsweetened shredded coconut
- 1 tablespoon unsweetened almond milk

Possible Variations:
Swap peanut butter with almond butter for a different nutty flavor. If you prefer a touch of sweetness, add a teaspoon of stevia or monk fruit sweetener.

Preparation:
1. Mix all the ingredients in a bowl until a thick dough forms.
2. Press the dough evenly into a parchment-lined small tray.
3. Refrigerate for at least 30 minutes until firm.
4. Cut into 6 bars and enjoy as a high-protein, on-the-go snack.

Nutritional Info (per serving): kcal 210 | pro 15g | carbs 8g | fat 14g

---

Blueberry Almond Greek Yogurt Tart Temptation

Servings: 1 tart (yields 4 slices)

Prep Time: 10 minutes (plus 15 minutes chilling)

Ingredients:
- 1/2 cup almond flour
- 1 tablespoon melted coconut oil
- 1 teaspoon vanilla extract
- 3/4 cup plain Greek yogurt
- 1/2 cup fresh blueberries

Possible Variations:
Swap blueberries for raspberries or strawberries, or drizzle almond butter on top for added richness.

Preparation:
1. Mix almond flour, melted coconut oil, and vanilla extract in a bowl until a crumbly crust forms.
2. Press the crust mixture evenly into a small tart pan and refrigerate for 10–15 minutes to set.
3. Spread the Greek yogurt evenly over the crust.
4. Top with fresh blueberries and chill for another 10 minutes before slicing and serving.

Nutritional Info (per serving, 1 slice): kcal 180 | pro 15g | carbs 10g | fat 10g

Strawberry Coconut Cream Dream Cups

Servings: 2 cups

Prep Time: 5 minutes

Ingredients:
- 1/2 cup unsweetened coconut cream
- 1/2 cup fresh strawberries, diced
- 1/2 teaspoon vanilla extract
- 1 teaspoon unsweetened shredded coconut (for garnish)

Preparation:
1. Mix coconut cream, diced strawberries, and vanilla extract in a bowl until smooth.
2. Divide the mixture into two small serving cups.
3. Sprinkle shredded coconut on top and serve immediately.

Possible Variations:
For a refreshing twist, add a squeeze of lime juice. If you prefer a sweeter flavor, mix in a teaspoon of stevia or monk fruit sweetener.

Nutritional Info (per serving): kcal 200 | pro 2g | carbs 10g | fat 18g

Mocha Protein Mousse Magic

Servings: 1 person

Prep Time: 5 minutes (plus 10 minutes chilling)

Ingredients:
- 1/2 cup unsweetened almond milk
- 1 scoop chocolate protein powder
- 1/2 teaspoon instant coffee granules
- 1/2 teaspoon vanilla extract
- 1 teaspoon unsweetened cocoa powder

Preparation:
1. Blend all the ingredients until smooth and creamy.
2. Transfer the mousse into a serving bowl.
3. Refrigerate for 10 minutes to allow the flavors to set.
4. Stir before serving and enjoy this rich, high-protein dessert.

Possible Variations:
If you like a stronger coffee flavor, increase the instant coffee granules to 1 teaspoon. For a richer consistency, swap almond milk with unsweetened coconut cream.

Nutritional Info (per serving): kcal 180 | pro 22g | carbs 8g | fat 6g

FAQ

When starting a high-protein, low-carb diet, it's natural to have questions. You might be wondering if you're eating the right balance of nutrients, if you're doing something wrong when you don't see immediate results, or how to handle certain situations like dining out or dealing with cravings.

This section is designed to clear up common doubts and help you stay confident in your journey. My goal is to make this process simple, enjoyable, and stress-free, so you can focus on feeling great, staying energized, and reaching your goals.

Below, you'll find answers to some of the most common concerns that people have when following this way of eating.

FAQ – Common Questions & Answers

1. **Will I feel tired when cutting carbs?**
   It's possible to feel a bit sluggish at first, especially if your body is used to running on a high-carb diet. This is called the low-carb flu, and it usually lasts a few days. Staying hydrated, increasing electrolyte intake (sodium, potassium, and magnesium), and eating enough healthy fats and proteins can help.
2. **Can I build muscle on a high-protein, low-carb diet?**
   Absolutely! Protein is essential for muscle growth and recovery. As long as you consume enough protein and maintain a consistent strength-training routine, you can build muscle while following this diet.
3. **How do I know if I'm eating enough protein?**
   A general rule is to aim for 0.7 to 1 gram of protein per pound of body weight, depending on your activity level. If you're unsure, track your intake using a food diary or an app to make sure you're meeting your protein needs.
4. **What if I don't see results right away?**
   Weight loss and body composition changes take time. Your body might be adjusting, holding onto water weight, or building muscle while losing fat. Stay consistent, focus on how you feel, and take progress photos instead of relying only on the scale.
5. **Can I eat carbs sometimes?**
   Yes! This is a low-carb diet, not a no-carb diet. Depending on your personal needs, you can

include healthy, fiber-rich carbs like vegetables, berries, and small portions of whole grains while still seeing progress.

6. **What should I do if I get cravings for sweets or junk food?**
Cravings are normal, but they often go away when you nourish your body with enough protein and healthy fats. If you still crave something sweet, try one of the light desserts from this book, have a high-protein snack, or drink a glass of water—sometimes thirst is mistaken for hunger.

7. **Is this diet safe for long-term health?**
Yes! A well-balanced high-protein, low-carb diet that includes nutrient-dense whole foods (lean proteins, healthy fats, and fiber-rich veggies) is not only safe but can improve metabolic health, energy levels, and overall well-being.

8. **How can I stay on track when eating out at restaurants?**
Look for protein-based dishes like grilled meats, fish, or eggs, and pair them with non-starchy vegetables instead of high-carb sides. Many restaurants allow substitutions—don't hesitate to ask for a salad instead of fries or for sauces/dressings on the side.

9. **Can I drink alcohol on this diet?**
Yes, but in moderation. Stick to low-carb options like dry wine, whiskey, vodka, or tequila (without sugary mixers). Keep in mind that alcohol can slow down weight loss and may increase cravings for high-carb foods.

10. **How do I meal prep efficiently for the week?**
The key is batch cooking and simplicity. Grill or bake proteins in advance, cook a batch of vegetables, and prepare a few easy sauces or dressings. That way, you can mix and match ingredients to create different meals throughout the week.

11. **Will I lose weight even if I don't count calories?**
Many people naturally lose weight on a high-protein, low-carb diet because it reduces hunger and cravings. However, if you hit a plateau, tracking calories and macros for a short time can help you understand your intake better.

12. **Can I still enjoy snacks between meals?**
Absolutely! High-protein, low-carb snacks like nuts, cheese, boiled eggs, or Greek yogurt can keep you satisfied between meals and prevent overeating later. Check out the Stress-Free Snacks section for more ideas.

13. **What if my family doesn't want to follow this diet?**
That's okay! Many of the meals in this book are family-friendly and delicious for everyone, even those not following the diet. You can always adjust portion sizes or add extra carbs (like rice or potatoes) to their plates while keeping yours low-carb.

14. **What should I do if I fall off track?**
Don't panic! One meal or even a day off plan won't ruin your progress. The most important thing is to get back on track with your next meal instead of feeling guilty or giving up. Progress is about consistency, not perfection.

15. **I don't have much time to cook. Can I still do this diet?**
Yes! That's exactly why this book is designed around quick and easy meals. With smart grocery shopping and simple meal prepping, you can put together healthy meals in 30 minutes or less.

16. **Can I modify these recipes for my personal needs?**
Definitely! The recipes in this book offer ingredient variations, so you can swap foods based on allergies, preferences, or dietary restrictions. Feel free to experiment and make the meals work for you!

Tips on Calorie and Macronutrient Tracking

When I first started my high-protein, low-carb journey, I was obsessed with numbers—calories, macros, grams of this, percentages of that. I thought if I didn't track everything perfectly, I wouldn't see results. But let me tell you: it doesn't have to be that complicated.

Yes, understanding calories and macronutrients (proteins, fats, and carbs) is important, especially if you have specific goals like losing weight, maintaining muscle, or optimizing your energy levels. But the key is learning how to track without driving yourself crazy.

Here's what I've learned along the way—simple, practical ways to track your intake without stress.

1. Start by Understanding What Your Body Needs

Before you start tracking, it helps to have a baseline idea of how much food your body actually needs. This depends on:

- Your age, height, and weight
- Your activity level (sedentary, active, highly active)
- Your specific goals (weight loss, muscle gain, maintenance)

A general starting point for a high-protein, low-carb diet:

- **Protein:** 0.7–1.0 grams per pound of body weight
- **Carbs:** Typically under 100g per day (or lower if following a stricter low-carb approach)
- **Fats:** The rest of your calories should come from healthy fats

If you're unsure where to start, online calorie calculators can give you a rough estimate of your total daily energy expenditure (TDEE) and suggest how many calories to eat for your goal.

2. Keep It Simple: Track Only What Matters

I used to think I had to log every bite of food, but the truth is—you don't need to track obsessively to see progress. Instead, focus on the key numbers that matter:

- **Protein intake** → This is the most important macronutrient in your diet, so make sure you're getting enough.
- **Carb intake** → Keeping this in check helps you stay within the high-protein, low-carb range.
- **Calories (only if necessary)** → If your goal is weight loss or muscle gain, keeping an eye on your daily intake can be helpful, but it's not mandatory for everyone.

If tracking everything overwhelms you, just start with protein. Most people don't get enough, and once you hit your protein target, everything else usually falls into place naturally.

3. Use Easy Tracking Methods

You don't need a spreadsheet or a complicated formula to keep track of what you eat. Here are three easy ways to make tracking effortless:

- **Use an app** – Apps like MyFitnessPal or Cronometer let you log meals quickly and save frequent foods.

Use hand-size portions – Instead of measuring everything, use this guide:

- **Protein:** A palm-sized portion of meat, fish, eggs, or tofu (about 20-30g of protein)
- **Fats:** A thumb-sized portion of olive oil, nuts, or avocado
- **Carbs:** A cupped hand of veggies or a small scoop of berries

Follow the plate method – Fill half your plate with protein, a quarter with non-starchy vegetables, and the rest with healthy fats. Simple and effective!

4. Learn to Estimate Without Measuring Everything

At first, I weighed and measured everything because I wanted to be 100% accurate. But after a few weeks, I realized I didn't need to. I had trained my eye to recognize portions.

Here's a trick: Spend one or two weeks measuring your portions to get a feel for what 30g of protein or 10g of carbs looks like. Then, you'll be able to eyeball portions without needing a scale every time.

For example:
- A chicken breast the size of your palm is roughly 30g of protein.
- A handful of nuts is about 1 serving of healthy fats.
- A small bowl of broccoli or leafy greens is a low-carb, fiber-rich side.

Once you get familiar with portion sizes, you can track intuitively instead of meticulously counting every calorie.

5. Be Flexible & Adjust as Needed

Your body isn't a robot, and neither is your appetite. Some days you'll be hungrier, some days less. And that's totally normal. Listen to your body, not just the numbers.

If you're hungry all the time, you might not be eating enough protein or healthy fats.

If you're not seeing results, check if you're overeating "healthy" high-calorie foods like nuts, cheese, or oils.

If you feel low on energy, experiment with adding a few more healthy carbs (like berries, quinoa, or sweet potatoes) and see how your body responds.

Tracking is a tool, not a rulebook. Use it to guide your choices, but don't let it stress you out.

6. What If You Don't Want to Track at All?

Good news: You don't have to. Many people follow a high-protein, low-carb diet successfully without tracking macros. The key is eating whole, nutrient-dense foods and sticking to basic meal structures:

- **Prioritize protein at every meal.**
- **Choose fiber-rich, non-starchy veggies to stay full.**
- **Include healthy fats like avocado, olive oil, nuts, and seeds.**

If you eat mindfully and consistently, you'll naturally stay within your target range without needing to track every gram.

FINAL ADVICE FOR LASTING CHANGE

You've come a long way. By now, you have all the tools you need to embrace a high-protein, low-carb lifestyle, create balanced meals, stay active, and build habits that support your health goals.

But if there's one thing I want you to take away from this journey, it's this:
This is not a short-term fix. It's a long-term way of living that will continue to evolve with you.

I know how easy it is to fall into the trap of wanting quick results—to see the number on the scale drop fast, to feel like every meal has to be perfect, or to assume that one slip-up means you've failed. But real, lasting change doesn't happen overnight. It happens through consistent, intentional actions taken day after day.

Embracing the Long-Term Mindset

One of the biggest shifts you need to make is understanding that this isn't about being "on" or "off" a diet—it's about finding a way of eating and moving that feels sustainable and enjoyable.

That means:
- Focusing on progress, not perfection. You don't need to eat perfectly or work out every day to succeed. What matters is consistency over time.
- Understanding that setbacks are normal. You will have days where you eat off-plan, skip a workout, or feel unmotivated. That's life. The key is to get back on track without guilt and keep moving forward.
- Letting go of the all-or-nothing mindset. One indulgent meal or a weekend off track does not erase all your progress. What matters is what you do most of the time, not what you do once in a while.

Maintaining Your Results Over Time

Once you've reached your initial goals—whether it's weight loss, muscle gain, or simply feeling better—it's important to shift your focus from results to maintenance. Many people struggle with this phase because they think they no longer need to be as mindful, but in reality, long-term success comes from continuing to apply the same principles.

Here are some ways to maintain your progress without feeling like you're constantly "dieting":
- **Keep meals simple and balanced.** You don't need to track everything forever, but it's helpful to continue prioritizing protein, fiber, and healthy fats in every meal.
- **Stay active in a way that feels good.** Exercise should never feel like punishment. Find ways to move your body that bring you joy—whether it's strength training, walking, yoga, or playing a sport.
- **Listen to your body.** As your lifestyle changes, so will your needs. Pay attention to hunger cues, energy levels, and how different foods make you feel. Adjust your diet accordingly instead of rigidly following a plan that no longer serves you.
- **Be flexible.** Life will always throw challenges your way—vacations, holidays, stressful periods. Instead of seeing them as obstacles, learn to navigate them with balance. You can enjoy social events, occasional indulgences, and changes in routine without losing progress.

Keep Learning and Growing

One of the most powerful things you can do for yourself is to continue expanding your knowledge. Health and nutrition are constantly evolving fields, and staying informed helps you make educated choices that align with your goals.

Here are some ways to keep learning and growing:

1. **Follow reputable nutrition and fitness experts.** Not all information on the internet is reliable. Seek guidance from qualified professionals who base their advice on science, not trends.
2. **Experiment with what works best for you.** Every person's body responds differently. Don't be afraid to tweak your approach—whether it's adjusting your macronutrient intake, trying new workouts, or finding different ways to stay active.
3. **Join a supportive community.** Whether it's an online group, a local fitness class, or a network of like-minded friends, having support makes a huge difference in staying motivated and accountable.
4. **Set new goals.** Once you've achieved your initial milestones, keep challenging yourself. Maybe you want to build more muscle, run a 5K, or simply feel more energized every day. Having something to work toward keeps you engaged and excited about your journey.

You Are in Control of Your Journey

At the end of the day, you are in charge of your health, your habits, and your mindset. There will always be distractions, challenges, and moments of doubt. But the power to stay on track, to adapt, and to keep moving forward is entirely in your hands.

If you take anything from this book, let it be this:
- Trust yourself and your ability to make lasting changes.
- Be patient with the process, and remember that results come from consistency, not perfection.
- Enjoy the journey—because taking care of yourself is one of the greatest gifts you can give yourself.

You have everything you need to succeed.
Now, go live the lifestyle that makes you feel strong, confident, and unstoppable.

EXTRA RESOURCES

One of the biggest lessons I've learned on this journey is that having the right tools and resources can make all the difference. When I first started, I often felt overwhelmed—unsure of what to eat, how to track my progress, or how to stay motivated when life got busy. But over time, I found simple, practical resources that kept me organized, inspired, and on track without feeling like I was forcing myself into a rigid routine.

This section includes some of the most useful tools that helped me stick with my high-protein, low-carb lifestyle while making the process feel easy and enjoyable. Whether it's a quick conversion chart for measurements, a basic grocery list, a ready-to-use 30-day meal plan, or even just a space for you to jot down notes and reflections, these are the exact resources that made my journey feel effortless and fun.

I hope they do the same for you!

Conversion Charts

When following recipes, especially if you're experimenting with different ingredients or adjusting portion sizes, having a reliable set of conversion charts can save you time and guesswork.

Whether you need to switch between grams and ounces, cups and tablespoons, or find the right cooking temperature conversion, this guide will help you stay on track without frustration.

Basic Measurement Conversions	
Liquids:	
1 tablespoon	15 ml
1 cup	240 ml
1 pint	473 ml
1 liter	4.2 cups
Dry Ingredients:	
1 ounce	28 grams
1 pound	454 grams
1 cup of almond flour	~96 grams
1 cup of coconut flour	~128 grams
1 cup of shredded cheese	~128 grams

Protein Portion Guide

Protein-rich foods can vary in density and weight, so here's a quick reference for estimating portion sizes without needing a scale.

1 small chicken breast	~4 oz (113g) = ~26g protein
1 large egg	~6g protein
1 oz of lean beef	~7g protein
1 cup of Greek yogurt	~20g protein
1 oz of cheese	~6-7g protein

Oven Temperature Conversions

If you're following recipes from different sources, you may need to convert temperatures between Fahrenheit and Celsius.

300°F	150°C
325°F	163°C
350°F	177°C
375°F	190°C
400°F	204°C
425°F	218°C

Substituting Common Ingredients

Sometimes, you may need to swap out an ingredient due to availability, dietary restrictions, or personal preference. Here are some easy substitutions:

Almond flour	Coconut flour (Use 1/4 cup coconut flour for every 1 cup almond flour, but increase liquid)
Heavy cream	Coconut cream (1:1 ratio)
Sugar	Stevia or erythritol (Adjust based on sweetness preference)
Soy sauce	Coconut aminos (1:1 ratio)
Pasta	Zucchini noodles or spaghetti squash (1 cup cooked pasta ≈ 1.5 cups zoodles)

Final Thoughts on Using Conversion Charts

Having these quick conversions at your fingertips takes the stress out of cooking and meal prepping. Whether you're adjusting recipes, measuring portions, or trying new ingredients, these simple guides will help you stay accurate and confident in the kitchen.

Basic Grocery List

One of the easiest ways to set yourself up for success with a high-protein, low-carb lifestyle is to have a well-stocked kitchen. When you have the right ingredients on hand, making healthy meals becomes effortless, and you'll be far less tempted by processed foods or last-minute takeout.

This basic grocery list includes staple items that are widely available in the U.S. and can help you build delicious, protein-rich, low-carb meals with minimal effort.

Protein Sources

Protein is the foundation of this lifestyle, helping you stay full, build muscle, and support fat loss. These versatile, easy-to-cook options will cover all your needs.

Poultry	Chicken breast, chicken thighs, turkey breast, ground turkey
Beef	Lean ground beef (85%+ lean), sirloin, flank steak, ribeye
Pork	Pork chops, pork tenderloin, uncured bacon
Seafood	Salmon, tuna, shrimp, tilapia, cod
Eggs & Dairy	Whole eggs, egg whites, Greek yogurt (unsweetened), cottage cheese, cheese (cheddar, mozzarella, Parmesan, feta)
Plant-Based Protein	Tofu, tempeh, edamame

Low-Carb Vegetables

Vegetables provide fiber, vitamins, and antioxidants while keeping your meals fresh and flavorful. These low-carb options are perfect for sides, salads, and meal preps.

Leafy Greens	Spinach, kale, romaine lettuce, arugula
Cruciferous Veggies	Broccoli, cauliflower, Brussels sprouts, cabbage
Other Low-Carb Veggies	Bell peppers, zucchini, cucumbers, mushrooms, asparagus, green beans
Alliums for Flavor	Garlic, onions, shallots

Healthy Fats

Fats are essential for satiety and hormone balance. These healthy fat sources are great for cooking and adding flavor to meals.

Oils	Extra virgin olive oil, avocado oil, coconut oil
Avocado	
Nuts & Sedds	Almonds, walnuts, pecans, chia seeds, flaxseeds
Nut Butters	Almond butter, peanut butter (no added sugar)

Pantry Staples

These must-have items make cooking easier and add bold flavors to your meals without added sugars or unnecessary carbs.

Low-Carb Flours	Almond flour, coconut flour
Broths & Stocks	Chicken broth, beef broth, vegetable broth
Canned Goods	Tuna, salmon, coconut milk (unsweetened), diced tomatoes
Low-Carb Sauces & Condiments	Mustard, hot sauce, sugar-free ketchup, coconut aminos (as a soy sauce alternative)
Herbs & Spices	Garlic powder, onion powder, paprika, cumin, oregano, basil, cinnamon

Low-Carb Fruits

While most fruits are higher in carbs, these options can fit into a low-carb diet in moderation.

Berries	Strawberries, raspberries, blueberries, blackberries
Citrus	Lemons, limes
Others	Avocados, olives, coconut

Snacks & Quick Bites

For busy days, having grab-and-go options will keep you full and prevent you from reaching for unhealthy alternatives.

Cheese sticks
Hard-boiled eggs
Beef jerky (sugar-free)
Nuts & seeds
Hummus with veggies
Greek yogurt with nuts

Final Thoughts on Grocery Shopping

Sticking to this basic grocery list will make meal planning easier, faster, and stress-free.

By keeping your fridge and pantry stocked with high-protein, low-carb essentials, you'll always be ready to whip up a delicious, satisfying meal—even on your busiest days!

Seasonal Fruits & Vegetables Guide

Eating seasonal produce is one of the best ways to enjoy fresh, flavorful, and nutrient-dense foods while keeping your meals exciting and varied throughout the year. Seasonal fruits and vegetables are often more affordable, fresher, and richer in vitamins and minerals since they are harvested at peak ripeness.

This guide will help you choose low-carb fruits and vegetables that are in season throughout the year in the U.S., so you can always have the best ingredients on hand for your high-protein, low-carb lifestyle.

WINTER (DECEMBER – FEBRUARY)

During the colder months, root vegetables, cruciferous greens, and citrus fruits are at their best.

Vegetables in Season
Brussels sprouts
Cauliflower
Cabbage (green, red, Napa)
Kale
Spinach
Swiss chard
Broccoli
Turnips
Radishes
Carrots
Celery root
Mushrooms
Leeks
Low-Carb Fruits in Season
Lemons
Limes
Grapefruit
Oranges (moderation)
Cranberries (unsweetened, great for sauces)
Avocados

SPRING (MARCH – MAY)

Spring is when tender greens and fresh, crisp veggies start to flourish, making it a great time for light, refreshing meals.

Vegetables in Season
Asparagus
Artichokes
Radishes
Arugula
Spinach
Butter lettuce
Swiss chard
Green onions
Snap peas (in moderation)
Fennel
Low-Carb Fruits in Season
Strawberries
Raspberries
Lemons
Limes
Limes

SUMMER (JUNE – AUGUST)

Summer brings an abundance of vibrant, juicy, and fiber-rich produce, perfect for salads, grilling, and refreshing snacks.

Vegetables in Season
Zucchini
Yellow squash
Bell peppers
Cucumbers
Eggplant
Green beans

Tomatoes
Okra
Fresh herbs (basil, mint, cilantro, dill)
Low-Carb Fruits in Season
Blackberries
Blueberries
Raspberries
Strawberries
Peaches (in moderation)
Watermelon (in small amounts)
Cantaloupe (in small amounts)

FALL (SEPTEMBER – NOVEMBER)

As the weather cools, fall brings hearty vegetables and warm, comforting flavors to the table.

Vegetables in Season
Pumpkins (great for low-carb baking)
Butternut squash (moderation)
Spaghetti squash
Brussels sprouts
Broccoli
Cauliflower
Kale
Cabbage
Mushrooms
Beets (moderation)
Low-Carb Fruits in Season
Apples (in moderation, higher in carbs)
Pears (in moderation)
Cranberries
Pomegranates (small portions)
Figs (small portions)

Final Thoughts on Eating Seasonally

Incorporating seasonal produce into your meals makes it easy to enjoy fresh, nutrient-rich ingredients year-round. Not only does seasonal eating enhance flavor and variety, but it also helps you save money and support local farmers.

Whenever possible, try shopping at local farmers' markets or looking for seasonal labels at the grocery store. By choosing produce that's in season, you'll keep your high-protein, low-carb meals exciting, flavorful, and naturally nutritious all year long!

30-Days Meal Plan

One of the biggest challenges when transitioning to a high-protein, low-carb lifestyle is knowing exactly what to eat every day. Many meal plans are too rigid, repetitive, or don't teach you how to make adjustments based on real life.

That's why this 30-day meal plan is designed to be: Structured but flexible—Providing a clear daily guide while allowing ingredient swaps.

- **Varied and exciting—Using different meals across the weeks to avoid boredom.**
- **Time-saving—Incorporating meal prep strategies so you're not cooking from scratch every day.**
- **Realistic and sustainable—Including planned flex meals, so you can eat out and enjoy treats guilt-free.**

This plan teaches you how to eat for life, not just for 30 days. By the end, you'll know how to build balanced meals, handle social events, and create a sustainable routine that works for you.

WEEK 1: FOUNDATIONS & MEAL PREP BASICS

Goal: Get comfortable with high-protein, low-carb eating while keeping meals simple and easy.

WEEK 1	BREAKFAST	LUNCH	DINNER	SNACK
DAY 1	Sunrise Energy Omelette	Zesty Garden Chicken Wrap	Basil Lime Beef Quick-Bake with Roasted Zucchini	Greek Yogurt with Berries & Almonds
DAY 2	Almond Dream Pancakes	Spicy Shrimp Lunch Delight over Cauliflower Rice	Crispy Chicken Veggie Skillet	Cheese Sticks & Walnuts
DAY 3	Green Glow Egg Muffins	Avocado & Turkey Power Bowl	Teriyaki Turkey Stir-Fry	Nutty Seed Crunch Clusters
DAY 4	Supercharged Morning Smoothie Bowl	Greek Power Chicken Salad	Sizzling Steak & Pepper Medley	Hard-Boiled Eggs with Mustard Dip
DAY 5	Cottage Crunch Sunrise Bowl	Lean Beef Crunch Salad	Garlic Herb Salmon Surprise	Protein-Packed Cottage Cheese Medallions
DAY 6	Avocado Power Wrap	Ultimate Turkey Cobb Wrap	Chili Lime Chicken Fajitas	Crunchy Almond Energy Bites
DAY 7	Chia Charge Overnight Pudding	Fresh & Zesty Turkey Wrap Supreme	(Flex Meal) Steak with Roasted Potatoes & Steamed Asparagus	Smokin' Paprika Beef Jerky

NOTE:

_____

_____

_____

_____

_____

WEEK 2: EXPANDING VARIETY & FLAVOR

Goal: Try new recipes, adjust portion sizes, and experiment with different proteins.

WEEK 2	BREAKFAST	LUNCH	DINNER	SNACK
DAY 8	Fluffy Protein Pancake Sundae Surprise	Herb-Infused Chicken Zoodle Salad	Speedy Tofu & Veggie Curry	Greek Yogurt Berry Burst Cups
DAY 9	Nutty Berry Dream Yogurt	Tangy Mediterranean Olive Bites	Express Eggplant Parmesan Bake	Zesty Tuna Cucumber Cups
DAY 10	Radiant Avocado Egg Bowl	Chicken Caesar Snack Cups	Lightning Beef Zoodle Bowl	Cheddar Cauliflower Popper Bites
DAY 11	Mocha Protein Mousse Magic	Spicy Chicken Caesar Lettuce Cups	Hearty Chicken Caesar Bake	Mini Egg Salad Lettuce Wraps
DAY 12	Berry Burst Frozen Yogurt Jewels	Wholesome Tofu & Spinach Stir-Fry	Homestyle Turkey Veggie Roast	Tofu Satay Protein Nuggets
DAY 13	Vanilla Chia & Mixed Berry Symphony	Hearty Quinoa Veggie Wrap	Flash-Fried Beef & Broccoli	Crispy Baked Cinnamon-Kissed Pears
DAY 14	Choco-Banana Protein Ice Cream Delight	Protein-Packed Mediterranean Salad	(Flex Meal) Sushi (opt for sashimi and a roll with less rice)	Power Chia Pudding Poppers

NOTE:

_____

_____

_____

_____

WEEK 3: INTRODUCING FLEXIBILITY & SOCIAL MEALS

Goal: This week focuses on real-life situations—eating out, handling social gatherings, and learning how to enjoy flexibility without guilt. You'll still follow a high-protein, low-carb approach, but you'll also incorporate one flex meal per week where you allow yourself a little extra freedom.

A flex meal doesn't mean going overboard—it's about enjoying foods you love while maintaining balance. You'll see examples of how to navigate different situations like dining out, family gatherings, or drinks with friends, so you feel confident making choices that fit your lifestyle.

Flex Meal Example: Pizza - Drinks with Friends - Office Lunch or Work Event - Brunch with Family - Dessert after dinner - Dinner at a Friend's House - Family Celebration or Holiday Meal.

WEEK 1	BREAKFAST	LUNCH	DINNER	SNACK
DAY 15	Cottage Crunch Sunrise Bowl	Spicy Chicken Caesar Lettuce Cups	Chili Lime Chicken Fajitas	Greek Yogurt Berry Burst Cups
DAY 16	Nutty Berry Dream Yogurt	Fresh & Zesty Turkey Wrap Supreme	Homestyle Turkey Veggie Roast	Power Chia Pudding Poppers
DAY 17	Chia Charge Overnight Pudding	Herb-Infused Chicken Zoodle Salad	Garlic Herb Salmon Surprise	Smokin' Paprika Beef Jerky
DAY 18	Supercharged Morning Smoothie Bowl	Ultimate Turkey Cobb Wrap	Hearty Chicken Caesar Bake	Almond Butter with Celery Sticks
DAY 19	Fluffy Protein Pancake Sundae Surprise	Spicy Shrimp Lunch Delight	Speedy Tofu & Veggie Curry	Mini Egg Salad Lettuce Wraps
DAY 20	Mocha Protein Mousse Magic	Hearty Quinoa Veggie Wrap	Basil Lime Beef Quick-Bake	Tofu Satay Protein Nuggets
DAY 21	Avocado Power Wrap	Protein-Packed Mediterranean Salad	Sizzling Steak & Pepper Medley	Crispy Baked Cinnamon-Kissed Pears

WEEK 4: SUSTAINABLE EATING FOR LIFE

Goal: Build confidence in meal planning independently, make smart food choices without overthinking, and develop true long-term sustainability.

By this point, you've spent three weeks following a structured meal plan, learning how to prepare balanced meals, navigate social situations, and incorporate flex meals without guilt. Now, it's time to step into full independence—where you start making food decisions without feeling restricted or overwhelmed.

This week, you'll still follow a high-protein, low-carb structure, but with more flexibility to swap meals, experiment with new ingredients, and trust your own instincts.

How to Approach This Week

Plan your own meals using the framework from previous weeks.
You've already followed 21 days of structured meals—now it's time to start mixing and matching. If you loved a certain breakfast or dinner from previous weeks, repeat it! If you want to try something new, go for it.

Use the recipes in this book as inspiration but feel free to swap proteins, veggies, and healthy fats based on what you have on hand.

Keep meal prep simple and practical.
If you've enjoyed batch-cooking, keep it going. Pick one or two protein sources, two or three veggie options, and healthy fats to prepare ahead of time. This makes throwing together meals effortless during busy days.

Stick to your usual meal structure.
- Breakfast: High-protein meal to start your day.
- Lunch: Satisfying meal, possibly meal-prepped.
- Dinner: Balanced meal with protein, fiber, and healthy fats.
- Snack (optional): Something quick if needed.

Flex meals should remain controlled and intentional.
Continue allowing yourself one to two flex meals per week—but remember, flex meals don't mean overindulgence.

A flex meal is about enjoying food you love in moderation, not eating to excess.
If you have a higher-carb meal, balance it with a protein-rich, low-carb meal before or after to keep things steady.

This week is about transitioning from following a plan to making it your own. By now, you should feel:
- Confident in creating meals without overthinking.
- Comfortable making smart choices when dining out.
- Free from the mindset of "cheating" or "starting over."
- Able to balance indulgences while staying on track.

This isn't just a 30-day program—it's the foundation of a long-term, sustainable lifestyle.

If you continue eating this way 80-90% of the time, while allowing flexibility when needed, you'll maintain your results effortlessly and never feel like you're "on a diet" again.

You're in control. You have the tools. Now, go enjoy this lifestyle and make it truly yours!

How to Adjust the Plan for Your Needs

For Weight Loss:
Stick to lean proteins and non-starchy vegetables.
Reduce cheese, nuts, and oils if weight loss slows.

For Muscle Gain & Energy Boost:
Increase protein portions in each meal.
Add healthy carbs like quinoa, sweet potatoes, or berries in moderation.

For Convenience & Meal Prep:
Double portions and save leftovers.
Keep grab-and-go snacks like cheese sticks, boiled eggs, and jerky available.

Final Thoughts on the 30-Day Meal Plan
This plan is designed to be a practical guide—not a rigid diet. You now have a structured meal plan with 30 days of unique meals, but the goal is to use this as a learning tool to build your own balanced eating habits.

By the end of these 30 days, you'll:
- Feel more confident in choosing and preparing meals.

- Understand how to adjust portions and ingredients for your goals.
- Learn how to navigate social events & flex meals without guilt.
- Be ready to continue this lifestyle effortlessly.

This is your journey—make it work for you in a way that feels sustainable, enjoyable, and empowering.

BONUS

A Special Thank You & Your Exclusive Bonus Gifts

First of all, thank you!
From the bottom of my heart, I truly appreciate you for choosing this book and for taking the time to learn about the high-protein, low-carb lifestyle. My goal was to provide you with all the tools, recipes, and strategies you need to make this way of eating easy, enjoyable, and sustainable—and I sincerely hope it has helped you feel more confident and in control of your health journey.

If you've found value in this book, **I would love to hear your thoughts!**

Your review on **Amazon.com** doesn't just help me—it helps other readers make an informed choice and, most importantly, it helps people like you take a step toward a healthier lifestyle.

Two Exclusive Bonuses—Just for You!

To thank you for your time and support, I have prepared two exclusive bonus gifts that will take your results to the next level:

1. The Ultimate Meal Prep Guide – One of the biggest challenges people face when switching to a healthier lifestyle is time.

Between work, family, and daily responsibilities, it's easy to feel overwhelmed. That's why I created this step-by-step meal prep guide to show you how to:

- Save time in the kitchen by preparing multiple meals in advance.
- Make meal prep effortless with simple, high-protein, low-carb recipes that store well.
- Stay consistent even on busy days by always having nutritious meals ready.

2. The Activity Guide: Easy & Effective Workouts for a Healthier Life – Eating well is essential, but adding movement to your daily routine will amplify your results.

Whether you're new to exercise or looking for a way to stay active with minimal time commitment, this guide will help you:

- Incorporate quick, effective workouts even with a busy schedule.
- Learn the difference between strength training and cardio and which is best for you.
- Find simple at-home or gym-friendly workout routines that complement your diet.
- Discover natural supplements and how to choose the right protein powder for your needs.

How to Access Your Free Bonuses

Getting your free bonuses is super easy!
Just **scan the QR code** on this page and enter your email to receive both guides instantly in your inbox.

Stay in Touch!

I am always looking to improve and create valuable content, so if you have questions, feedback, or suggestions, feel free to reach out to me via email: **sarahhollins@bookbonus4u.com**

I would love to hear about your experience, what worked for you, and any ways I can make my future books even more helpful.

Thank you again for your trust!

Your health journey is just beginning, and I'm honored to be a small part of it. Keep going, stay consistent, and enjoy the process—you've got this!

Sarah Hollins

Space for Your Notes: Jot down your thoughts, feelings, any modifications you make to the recipes, or new recipes you create from scratch using your creativity.

© **Copyright 2025-2026 Sarah Hollins- All rights reserved.**

This document is geared towards providing exact and reliable information in regards to the topic and issue covered.
The publication is sold with the idea that the publisher is not required to render accounting, officially permitted, or otherwise, qualified services. If advice is necessary, legal or professional, a practiced individual in the profession should be ordered.

From a Declaration of Principles which was accepted and approved equally by a Committee of the American Bar Association and a Committee of Publishers and Associations.

In no way is it legal to reproduce, duplicate, or transmit any part of this document in either electronic means or in printed format. Recording of this publication is strictly prohibited and any storage of this document is not allowed unless with written permission from the publisher. All rights reserved.

The information provided herein is stated to be truthful and consistent, in that any liability, in terms of inattention or otherwise, by any usage or abuse of any policies, processes, or directions contained within is the solitary and utter responsibility of the recipient reader.

Under no circumstances will any legal responsibility or blame be held against the publisher for any reparation, damages, or monetary loss due to the information herein, either directly or indirectly.

Respective authors and publisher own all copyrights.
The information herein is offered for informational purposes solely, and is universal as so.
The presentation of the information is without contract or any type of guarantee assurance.

The trademarks that are used are without any consent, and the publication of the trademark is without permission or backing by the trademark owner.

All trademarks and brands within this book are for clarifying purposes only and are the owned by the owners themselves, not affiliated with this document.

Printed in Dunstable, United Kingdom